100 IDEAS
FOR SUPPORTING PUPILS ON
THE AUTISTIC SPECTRUM

100 IDEAS
FOR
SUPPORTING
PUPILS ON THE
AUTISTIC
SPECTRUM

Francine Brower

continuum

Continuum International Publishing Group
The Tower Building   80 Maiden Lane
11 York Road   Suite 704
SE1 7NX   New York, NY 10038

www.continuumbooks.com

British Library Cataloguing-in-Publication Data
A catalogue record for this book is available from the British
Library.

ISBN: 08264 94218 (paperback)

Library of Congress Cataloging-in-Publication Data
A catalog record for this book is available from the Library
of Congress.

Typeset by Ben Cracknell Studios | www.benstudios.co.uk
Printed and bound in Great Britain by Ashford Colour Press,
Gosport, Hampshire

CONTENTS

SECTION 3 **Developing social skills**

SECTION 4 **Creating the right environment**

SECTION 5 **Coping strategies**

SECTION 6 **Establishing foundations for learning**

SECTION 7 Tackling the curriculum

SECTION 8 Facing the challenge of change

INTRODUCTION

A decade or more ago most professionals working in mainstream schools were oblivious to the need to develop in-depth understanding of pupils with special educational needs. The autistic spectrum was not a term familiar to staff and if a pupil was identified with autism he was more than likely to be in a special school. Many individuals, of course, were not identified at all and were often left to cope in a world where they were sorely misunderstood and labelled as odd, difficult, uncooperative and/or learning disabled.

Much has changed over recent years. Many mainstream schools are seeking to include pupils who have a wide range of special educational needs, including pupils on the autistic spectrum. With heightened awareness comes heightened responsibility and it is essential that SENCOs, teachers and support staff recognize their need to understand the nature of the pupils they are supporting. The issues are complex. We need to understand how the pupil perceives the world – very differently from our own perceptions. To support a pupil on the autistic spectrum we must recognize the needs of the individual. Autistic spectrum disorders are lifelong disabilities that affect the way a person relates to the world. The presentation of the triad of impairments – communication, socialization and resistance to change – varies greatly from pupil to pupil, making it essential that staff are alert to and analyse the needs of each pupil as an individual.

This book will sketch a backdrop to the struggles faced by the pupil on the autistic spectrum. It will also address the needs with creative ideas to help staff understand and support the development of the pupil. A familiar phrase in educational circles is 'quality teaching first'. Ideas throughout this book will support your work with pupils on the autistic spectrum, but it is important to understand that the ideas presented are good practice for all pupils. In no way will the ideas be in conflict with the needs of the peer group.

My intention is that those using this book will gain a clearer understanding of the difficulties faced by the pupil and will recognize how, through increased understanding and awareness, they can enable full participation and enhance learning for pupils on the autistic spectrum. The ideas are not exhaustive but will act as signposts to encourage further reading, exploration and learning within the field of autism.

For the sake of simplicity the pupil will be referred to as 'he' or 'him'. This is not to say that females are not diagnosed with autistic spectrum disorders, but reflects the ratio of male to female of approximately 4:1 for autism and 9:1 for Asperger's syndrome.

Throughout the book the terms autistic spectrum disorder, ASD, autism and Asperger's syndrome will be used interchangeably. This recognizes the breadth of the spectrum as represented by individuals within our schools and services.

Enhancing understanding

GOOD PRACTICE FOR ALL

Some years ago I recommended visual strategies to a teacher of a Key Stage 2 pupil on the autistic spectrum. On my return to monitor the situation I was met with enthusiasm as she explained that she had developed the visual schedules for the entire class group and found everyone responding to and benefiting from this intervention. This experience has been repeated over the years as hosts of pupils are receiving benefits from the introduction of sound organizational strategies within the classroom.

Time consuming to introduce something new? Perhaps, in the short term. Time saving in organization and classroom management? Yes, in the long term. Supportive of the pupil on the autistic spectrum? Yes, definitely! Supportive of the peer group? Yes, without question! Implementation of ideas provided in this book to address the needs of pupils with autism will have a positive impact on quality teaching within the school environment.

Structure the day for the pupils in the same way that you structure your diary or day book for yourself. Just as you refer to your schedule to be prepared for what you are doing and what comes next, provide a schedule to enable the pupil to reference what the day or the session will hold. Have this information consistently ready, prominently displayed for the group at the front of the room or near the door and individually displayed next to the pupil's desk, and then he will develop the routine of checking when entering the room. The security this will provide will reduce unnecessary anxiety and enable the pupil to be supported through the predictability of the visual timetable.

The term inclusion is now a familiar one in education settings and raises both positive and negative responses from parents and professionals alike. Inclusion can be a positive experience for pupils on the autistic spectrum when it is properly resourced and when the school is prepared through training and whole-school understanding.

When pupils are included they feel secure, confident, accepted, valued, understood and at ease in the environment. Is this what your pupils on the autistic spectrum would say about their experiences within your school?

Throughout this book ideas will be presented that will help you provide a foundation of good practice to make your school a place where children and young people with autism feel included. The diagram below demonstrates the cycle that will enable success.

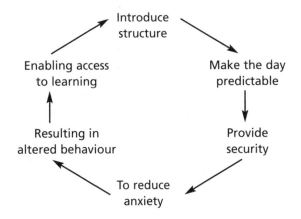

Introduce structure

Enabling access to learning

Make the day predictable

Resulting in altered behaviour

Provide security

To reduce anxiety

Use this cycle and your school can become an environment where inclusion is embedded, diversity is celebrated, individual disabilities are understood and all members of the school community are better prepared for their rightful place in society.

One of the features of autism is the lack of ability of the individual to generalize information from one context to another. For example, a pupil may learn to write his name with the blue pencil with Miss Smith's support. When the same task is presented with a yellow pencil he falters, not recognizing this pencil as the same 'tool' with the same function. Alternatively, the pencil may be the same, but the instruction is given by Mrs Wood, with a different set of words to prompt the task. To the pupil this is now a new and different task.

Within the secondary school context the pupil may learn to measure lines in mathematics and be very skilled and accurate in doing this. When the same skill is then required in art the pupil may be confused and behave as if the skill has not been previously introduced. Measurement, you see, has been associated with mathematics, but this is a new context, a new area of the curriculum, and the ruler may be a different length or made of a different material. The skill has not been generalized.

It is your role to help build the bridges to make these links. Demonstrate the familiar – the yellow pencil is the same as the blue. Generalize what a pencil is – long, short, with or without a rubber, various colours, thickness, and so on. What makes a pencil a pencil? Demonstrate its mark-making ability, show the pupil the lead. Similarly, demonstrate linear measure in a range of contexts with a range of tools, such as plastic, wooden and metal rulers, metre sticks, tape measures, and emphasize the purpose of the tool – to measure.

We take so much for granted. We instinctively know the relationship between items. But think – does the pupil recognize what the object is and what its function is? If not, plan specific activities for sorting and categorizing to help the pupil develop awareness of related sets of objects and words. Pick up on the child's confusion and demonstrate sameness to develop generalization. For example, if you say, 'Please shut the door' and the child does not respond, he may respond to, 'Please close the door' and you will then link the two words for him.

Our world is a very unpredictable place for individuals who experience anxiety when things around them are not the same and confusion prevails. A major challenge for a pupil on the autistic spectrum is coping with change. We can go some way to alleviate the anxiety by providing as much consistency as possible throughout the day and week.

What does consistency mean? As individuals in a supporting role (teachers, learning support assistants, learning mentors) it begins with our own day-by-day presentation – our mood, tone of voice, volume and level of tolerance will all have an effect on the pupil. This is magnified with respect to the peer group as, generally, young people are more prone to mood swings. Frequently, a child or young person with autism will prefer adult company because, for the most part, adults are more predictable and consistent.

In the same way that we expect to receive a consistent service from those managing us, we need to deliver consistent messages to our pupils. To this end, maintain an even temperament, deliver what has been agreed and warn the child of change. Make every effort to communicate clearly with the pupil and remember the need to develop and maintain a constant pattern of management throughout the day.

The key person supporting the pupil is often the mainstay in providing a consistent and predictable day. Other aspects relating to this topic will be addressed throughout the book.

CONSISTENCY – A MUST!

NEVER TAKE IT PERSONALLY

To work successfully with pupils on the autistic spectrum it is essential that you have an understanding of the communicative attempts and patterns of the pupil.

A major concern in schools is the management of behaviour when supporting pupils with autism. This may be behaviour that is deemed aggressive, for example, when a pupil hits or kicks out. Such behaviour is usually an attempt to communicate, even when we have failed to recognize the trigger for the behaviour. This understanding does not negate the fact that it hurt! It should, however, help staff to understand that it was not a targeted assault on the individual. Often, those with the closest relationship to the child are the recipients of the aggression, in part because the pupil has expected them to know what anxiety he was experiencing, to protect him from the situation, and they were unable to do this.

Similarly, when you speak to the pupil your words will be interpreted literally and you can expect a frank and honest reply! For example, you may be told that you have a big nose, a spot on your face or that your breath smells. As one Asperger's pupil said to a teacher, 'How do you expect me to learn from you when you have dandruff on your shoulders?' *Don't take it personally!* (Of course, you could sort out the dandruff as well!)

Do, however, provide the support to help the pupil understand why the behaviour and the comments are offensive and hurtful to others. Teach the rules of what is acceptable in a supportive, factual, visual way such as:

Happy?	*Sad?*
I like your bag.	Your nose is big.

Create a list of negative and positive words and actions, and work with the pupil to identify which side of the chart they should be placed on. A neutral column may also be useful.

You will have learned a great deal throughout life in an incidental way. We can't easily identify how we learned our social understanding, the way we alter our language and the way we present ourselves in different contexts. Some of this has been by example, a great deal by being alert and watching, and some, it would seem, by 'osmosis'.

This is one of the challenges for individuals on the autistic spectrum. They may not have accumulated learning along the way. They have not built an understanding from the foundation up. It is our role to recognize this gap and address it.

How do we do this? When you are working to support a pupil on the autistic spectrum you must have your antennae ready to identify gaps in learning and understanding. This may be general knowledge or social relationships. When a gap is recognized take the time to explain the facts, make the links, and attempt to help the pupil generalize from information he already has.

Let me give you an example. A young man pushed between a colleague and me as we were standing in the doorway to the classroom. The teacher stopped him (politely), asked him to reverse, explained that we were speaking and that he needed to pause and say, 'Excuse me, please.' He put his hand to his forehead and replied, 'Oh, I didn't know that. Excuse me.' And we parted to let him enter the room. Too often our response is to scold and expect the pupil to alter his behaviour without a clear explanation of what is appropriate. Take the time to respond to the 'teaching moment' by helping the pupil replay the event and repeat it in a more acceptable way by modelling the improved behaviour.

REDUCING STRESS

Our world is not a comfortable or familiar one for pupils on the autistic spectrum. It creates high anxiety by the very nature of the unpredictability of daily events and the flexibility that most of us find so easy to cope with.

As a consequence, stress is a common experience shared by our pupils. It must be recognized that many young people on the autistic spectrum work very hard to control anxiety throughout the school day, with the result that the arrival at home triggers a 'melt down'. Too often, professionals fail to believe the problems described by parents and hold them responsible.

What causes anxiety? It is frequently the result of changes in routine, such as the bus being late, having a supply teacher, a key member of staff being absent, the behaviour of peers, forgetting to bring the right book or materials, the pace of lessons, an increase in volume, sensory overload and so on. But all day long the pupil bottles up the anxiety and becomes more and more stressed. Eventually it becomes too much and may escalate into misunderstood and unacceptable behaviour in school or on arrival home.

Being aware of this makes us responsible for:

○ watching for signs of stress and reassuring the pupil
○ providing a way out when demands or the environment are overwhelming – a break card (see example) or a safe haven to retreat to with permission

---

I need a break.
May I please leave the room?

○ liaising closely with parents to learn how stress is managed at home
○ providing discrete sessions to help the pupil develop coping strategies to deal with stress – for example, relaxation techniques such as a stress ball or deep breathing.

If we are aware of the struggles the young person is facing and we do not find ways to offer support, we are adding to the anxiety.

Some time ago when listening to a presentation given by an adult with Asperger's syndrome, this phrase struck me, 'All we ask you to do is to meet us halfway.' If only it were so easy!

What does this actually mean? We expect our pupils to conform, to follow the rules, to receive instructions and support and to be churned out with acceptable SATs results. When an individual doesn't see the world through our eyes *we* struggle to make the necessary adjustments.

It seems so much easier to adapt the environment for special educational needs related to physical disabilities – a barrier-free school and personal care plans are now quite readily accepted in our society. But how do we provide a barrier-free school for pupils with autism? How do we meet them halfway?

Ideally, by raising awareness through whole-school understanding and sharing information about the individual pupil with *all* staff. This understanding will help to avoid unnecessary confrontation and to create a flexible environment. Rather than making the staff aware of the deficits and weaknesses, recognize strengths. Although communication may be difficult, find ways to listen to the pupil, using his mode of communication to enable his voice to be heard.

Each of these issues will be further addressed in later sections of this book. Application of this principle, however, is vital. The adults in the situation must recognize how they can offer compromise and meet the pupil halfway.

MISINTERPRETATION

When you find communication and socialization difficult to navigate it is not unusual to struggle in interpreting others appropriately. Body language, tone of voice, facial expression, gesture and intent may be misinterpreted by our pupils and lead to what appears to be overreaction.

Why and how does this happen? An example may illustrate this. It is not unusual for a member of staff to reprimand a pupil and send him to the office. Let's call our pupil Adam. Adam then responds, 'It wasn't me. It isn't fair.' And he storms along the corridor with a face like thunder. Approaching him is John. John has Asperger's syndrome and as he sees Adam approaching he is anxious about his demeanour, assumes Adam is angry with him and pushes Adam in response to *anticipated* aggression.

Why did John do that? He doesn't have the skill to ask Adam what's wrong or to infer that Adam is on the way to the headteacher's office and therefore must be in trouble. Adam appeared to be a threat and John responded accordingly.

Likewise, a teacher may raise her voice in response to the volume in the classroom, but John reacts as if the raised voice is a personal threat to him or that he has done something wrong and he may then retaliate.

Once we have recognized the possibility of the pupil misinterpreting what is happening around him, it is vital that we explain incidents clearly, role-play strategies to use, model appropriate responses and give the pupil the tools to understand better the actions of others. In the above example, take time to role-play the incident in the corridor, playing the part of Adam, explaining the background of the incident and showing John how to leave a wide berth and pass by without comment or incident.

VULNERABILITY

Children and young people with autistic spectrum disorders are often vulnerable within their peer group and may become the target for pranks or, more seriously, bullying. The somewhat eccentric behaviour of some, the naivety of others and taking people at their word can leave the pupil open to abuse.

For example, a young person may respond to, 'I'll be your friend if . . . .' The 'if' may be 'if you steal a packet of crisps for me' or 'if you call Mr Barker a prat'. If the pupil wants a friend he will respond. Does he gain a friend? No, probably not. Does he get into trouble? Almost certainly.

We have a responsibility to teach these pupils to realize when their peers are a threat and to understand when others are not genuine in their intentions. This is complicated by the fact that pupils with ASD do not readily generalize situations and do misinterpret intentions. Thus, they can have increased vulnerability.

How do we address this issue? There must be time within the curriculum to role-play potential situations and to reinforce rules that are non-negotiable, for example, stealing, lying and physical assault are never acceptable behaviour.

At the heart of this is making sure that staff understand and are aware of the problems, identifying the potential for vulnerability, organizing activities, watching out for the pupil during unstructured, unsupervised times of the day and taking the time to debrief when a situation has occurred.

Where possible, develop a small group of supportive peers who will take an interest in the pupil, watch out for him and provide positive role models for acceptable behaviour. One example of this in a primary setting is for a group of willing peers to have their names on laminated strips and the pupil chooses one each day in turn throughout the week. This enables the group to play with others on four of the five days but always ensures that the pupil with ASD will have someone helping him to interact during play. In secondary school the development of a 'circle of friends' may be more appropriate. The ideas in Section 5 will look at this theme in more detail.

CHAMPION THE CAUSE

In my experience the pupils with ASD who are most successfully placed in mainstream settings are those who have a member of staff committed to understanding the nature of the pupil's needs and representing these needs to others. One enthusiastic individual who is willing to learn, analyse difficulties when they arise and use creative solutions to support the pupil can make an immense difference.

To be successful in this role you must:

○ like and accept the pupil(s) you are supporting
○ identify your ongoing training needs
○ seek information on ASD from every possible source:
  – websites
  – helplines
  – publications
  – courses
  – peer support
  – critical friend
  – professional interest group (if there isn't one in your local authority, be the pioneer to begin one)
  – others who know the pupil well, such as staff, parents, professionals.

As you work with the pupil always consider the challenges and difficulties that arise in light of the triad of impairments and possible sensory impact. You can become the person who makes the difference for the pupil in his short- and long-term development.

Whether you are working in a primary or secondary school context it is vitally important that *all* staff working with the pupil on the autistic spectrum have an understanding of the pupil's needs. 'All' includes management, teachers, learning support assistants, learning mentors, lunchtime organizers, the caretaker and anyone else who will come into regular contact with the pupil. This is the only way to achieve a consistent approach throughout the school.

One way to help with this understanding is to develop a pen portrait of the pupil. It is unlikely that many of the aforementioned will read files of material. However, if a succinct overview of the pupil is provided as part of whole-school training, it will enable everyone to see the main areas of support required.

The pen portrait should include:

Strengths	Weaknesses
Likes	Dislikes
Communication	Socialization
Prompts needed	Causes of stress
Sensory issues	Key person

Discussion in a staff session to emphasize the need for consistency and to remind staff of the main issues facing a child with autism will help to ensure that the portrait is understood. Remember, when a new staff member joins the school the process must be introduced again.

Enabling communication

PUTTING COMMUNICATION IN CONTEXT

We often make the assumption that communication is the art of speaking. In reality, our communication is a combination of gesture, body language, facial expression, tone of voice and context. Pupils on the autistic spectrum can have major difficulties with communication and a paramount goal must be to enable communication as a way to open up understanding and reduce frustration.

At one end of the spectrum the pupil may have no awareness of communication, no tools to interact and make needs known. At this stage of development it will be necessary to use objects of reference to assist the pupil, for example, a cup to indicate drink, a placemat to indicate dinnertime or a coat to indicate playtime. As he begins to respond to these concrete references the object can be accompanied with a photograph. If/when the photograph becomes understood it can be displayed with a representative symbol, enabling access to the commercially produced symbols that can support the visual timetable and daily structure. One strategy that has been successfully used to support two-way communication with individuals on the autistic spectrum is the Picture Exchange Communication System (PECS). Training and advice in this approach is available across the UK. In the fullness of time, if/when the pupil is able to benefit from text, the symbols can be presented with text and finally, if literacy develops, text can be used to communicate with him.

Throughout the process, each stage is augmented by appropriate levels of language, from individual words to key words to more standard language if it is understood.

If we do not recognize the appropriate stage of communication, we bombard our pupils with confusing speech that not only fails to get the message across, but also creates confusion and frustration that can lead the pupil to opt out.

We don't always realize how quickly we receive language, process it and then respond to what we have heard. Consequently we don't usually stop to think about how others process language. For pupils on the autistic spectrum this can be an enormous barrier to following the thread of what is going on around them.

Some have suggested that it takes an individual on the spectrum six seconds to process the spoken word. In testing this out with a pupil I found a ten-second lag from the end of my question to the beginning of his reply. Think about this, ask yourself a question, and time ten seconds on your watch before you give the answer. Do we ever allow anywhere near this time for processing? What we actually do is to quickly rephrase the instruction. For example:

> *'Put your pencils down please.' (Processing delay,*
> *put . . . your . . . pencils . . .)*
> *'I said, put your pencils down.' (Processing begins*
> *again, I . . . said . . . put . . .)*
> *'I am not going to tell you again.' (Processing begins*
> *again, I . . . am . . . not . . .)*

The pupil has not had the chance to get to the end of one instruction before the next one begins. Success is not possible.

In part, this demonstrates why it is often necessary for a young person with autism to have additional support, someone to 'interpret' for him. But this is not always possible and when it is not it is important for us to remember to gain the pupil's attention first, articulate clearly and, whenever possible, demonstrate visually what we are instructing him to do. In the example above, have a pencil in your hand and demonstrate putting it on the desk as the instruction is given.

PROCESSING TIME

UNDERSTANDING IDIOMS

Our language is rich with idioms and phrases that we use regularly, assuming that they are understood through the context of our conversation. This is another stumbling block for pupils on the autistic spectrum. One of my pupils once said to me, 'I used to think that when someone said the penny dropped I should look for it on the floor. Now I know it means "I understand".'

This example is the key to success. You should not stop using idioms as part of speech, but you must take the time to explain their meaning to the pupil. Expand his knowledge by working on idioms to help him work through the confusion that would otherwise be there. One way to address this is to introduce a range of idioms and have the pupils illustrate the literal meaning and write the actual meaning, thus emphasising the humour found in the language. For example, 'It's raining cats and dogs.'

It's raining cats and dogs

This means the rain is very heavy and the ground is getting very wet. There will be big puddles on the ground.

Think how often teachers use terms such as, 'It's as easy as pie', 'Don't bite off more than you can chew',

I'm all ears

'You made it by the skin of your teeth', 'Keep an eye on what you're doing', 'I want your eyes and ears'. Now think about these idioms and interpret them literally. Try to think about what meaning is conveyed if you truly take things literally and are unable to interpret the meaning. This is what your ASD pupils face. Help them to understand what our ambiguous and colourful language means.

Why is it that we are often negative in the way we respond to children? Imagine yourself leaving a friend's house and forgetting your umbrella. Your friend shouts to you as you go down the path, 'Can't you remember anything? You've left your umbrella. Honestly! I don't know about you!' It just wouldn't happen, would it? Well, I hope not.

Sadly, we too frequently hear this type of berating in schools and, even if it isn't quite so forceful, our natural instinct is to use the negative. For example, 'No running', 'Stop talking', 'Stop messing about', 'Can't you sit still?' When we make lists of school rules they are frequently presented in the negative.

The problem with this way of doing things is that we don't actually tell the pupil what *to* do. By thinking of the positive we are actually enabling the child to change his behaviour. Consider these changes:

○ No running becomes *walk safely*.
○ Stop talking becomes *work quietly*.
○ Stop messing about becomes *sit up and listen*.
○ Can't you sit still becomes *sit sensibly*.

You could even try a please and thank you at the beginning and the end!

THE POWER OF POSITIVE SPEAKING

REPAIRING CONVERSATIONS

When an individual is baffled by communication he often struggles to have the courage to initiate or respond to conversation. Lack of confidence can result in abbreviated sentences or low volume. This then makes it difficult to be understood and the person listening will fail to get the message and ask for it to be repeated. The fact that it was an effort to speak in the first place will often result in the pupil not wanting to 'repair' the conversation.

Another difficulty is that a pupil on the autistic spectrum will begin to speak without first gaining the attention of the person to whom he is speaking. Again, the conversation breaks down and when the listener asks for the comment to be repeated the pupil will be reluctant to do this.

This is a common problem and we often allow the conversation to end at that point. This does not address the issue or support the young person. When such a situation arises, explain that you did not hear the comment and that you would like to hear it. Allow time for the pupil to regain composure, encourage him to repeat what was said and *praise* the communicative effort. By doing this the pupil will begin to learn that it is fine to repeat what has been missed and it will demonstrate that *communication gets results*.

Throughout each school day teachers, learning support assistants, other members of staff and peers are dispensing information, giving instructions and carrying on conversations. There are times when each of us fails to get a message because we are unfamiliar with the vocabulary or take something literally that was meant otherwise. For the pupil on the autistic spectrum taking things literally can prove to be a barrier to learning and a trigger for misunderstanding.

Some examples may help to clarify this. A secondary teacher, trying to settle the class at the start of the lesson, was being inundated with questions from a pupil with Asperger's syndrome. He looked directly at the lad and said, 'Sit down!' The pupil sat down, where he was, on the floor. He failed to recognize the implied instruction, that is, to *go to his seat* and sit down. Similarly, if you ask a pupil if he knows where the office is while holding out the register the pupil will likely respond 'Yes', without realizing that the question implies that he should take the register to the office. When a teacher poses the question, 'Would you like to take out your books?' and the pupil responds, 'No', he is not being intentionally cheeky. He is giving an honest answer.

School is often a minefield for pupils with autism and we so often fail to see where we have gone wrong. When we ask everyone to stand the pupil may not realize that 'everyone' refers to him. Try to preface instructions by using the pupil's name and teach him that terms like 'everyone' and 'someone' include him.

How can you support understanding? Try to present information and ask questions in such a way that your message is clearly understood. Watch for situations where the pupil has misinterpreted the situation and explain what was actually meant.

CALLING A SPADE A SPADE

In Idea 5 the issue of not taking comments personally was discussed. Let's look at this in a little more detail. We expect the unwritten social rules to be understood by our pupils. We expect a measure of respect from pupils with whom we work. We know that pupils will 'take the mick' behind our backs, just like we did when we were in school. So, when a pupil fails to fit into this social code and speaks with complete honesty we struggle to understand why.

In the same way that pupils with autism understand language literally, they use language literally. If you have a spot on your face and the pupil points this out, it is purely a fact. You may find any number of physical features described in an honest and candid manner. For the pupil this is not an insult; it is simply a comment. One of the greatest difficulties is the reaction of peers who do understand the unwritten social conventions and who may delight in the comments if they are directed at staff.

This is another area that has to be addressed directly. Follow up the insult with an objective explanation of why it was not appropriate. Help the young person to recognize that some things he says are hurtful and explain what hurtful means. It is only through addressing the problem that it can begin to be solved. Reprimanding, giving detentions, reacting as if the comments are meant to hurt will not help the pupil to cope in similar situations in the future.

Pupils on the autistic spectrum vary greatly in both their ability in conversation and interest in it. For some pupils you may feel that they talk too much, while others seldom express themselves verbally.

Those who talk incessantly may focus on a particular topic of special interest. If the pupil is passionate about trains, for example, he will deliver large amounts of detailed information on the subject. Others may seldom initiate conversation and only respond with monosyllabic answers.

In both of these situations there are difficulties with dialogue, with shared conversation. The one dominates and fails to recognize the need for a communicative partner. The other seeks to withdraw from the demands of dialogue.

How do we support development of this skill?

○ Organize time away from busy classrooms to focus on opportunities to take turns in conversation.

○ Give specific rules related to dialogue – explain that both parties take turns, pause, use eye contact, gesture and so on.

○ Role-model conversations that have appropriate turn-taking, pauses and responses.

○ Encourage expanded sentences for reluctant conversationalists by demonstrating a more complete answer.

○ Use written conversations, writing a question and asking the pupil to respond in writing. This may be done on paper or on a computer.

○ When conversations go wrong, take the time to show the pupil how to improve.

DEVELOPING DIALOGUE

The term 'pupil voice' has become a common theme in recent years as schools are encouraged to help young people participate in school life and express their opinions on many issues. This is often very difficult for pupils on the autistic spectrum. When communication is impaired and conversations are difficult, alongside the issues of literal understanding and a frequent lack of confidence, how do we promote self-advocacy?

To achieve this, choose a comfortable environment with as few distractions as possible. Select a member of staff to act as a facilitator with whom the pupil has an established relationship. Present questions in an accessible way, remembering that visual presentation may be more helpful than verbal. When working with non-verbal pupils, use visual prompts, such as photographs or symbols, enabling the pupil to select the preferred answer. Always allow time for the pupil to process his response, prompting him as necessary, without putting words in his mouth. The member of staff should offer to be the scribe if this is helpful.

Struggling with communication should not take away the rights and opportunities for pupils on the autistic spectrum to have a voice in their education. Our challenge is to be creative in enabling their voices to be heard.

Developing social skills

TEACH THE SKILLS

Idea 6 looked at incidental learning – those things that we all know 'just because we know them'. As children, most of us knew when we had crossed the boundary merely from a firm look from a parent or a teacher. But what if you had not learned by this process of 'osmosis'? What if you had to be taught all the rules of social conventions and you missed the lessons? What if everyone else knew how to respond, what the joke was, what the expression on the teacher's face meant, except you? This is what pupils on the autistic spectrum face every day.

We cannot leave the learning of social skills to chance. They must be taught as a discrete part of the curriculum. Once taught they must be generalized across the school day and in other environments. In addition to direct teaching it is essential that social 'gaffs' are watched for and explained at the time, demonstrating the right way to improve on the situation in the future.

There are some misconceptions about inclusion leading to some schools failing to recognize the need to alter the curriculum to address the special needs of the pupil. On the contrary, the curriculum has to be altered. When a child is identified with an autistic spectrum disorder and requires discrete teaching of skills to improve communication and social understanding, time must be found to address these needs.

Look at the timetable and select opportunities to enhance these areas of need. Provide one-to-one time at the start of the day to remind the pupil of previous sessions and set some targets for the day ahead. Alternatively, take time at the end of the day to review what the day has entailed and ensure that targets are set for the following day. This would also enable communication with the pupil's home.

TRIGGERS FOR BEHAVIOUR

I have often heard the protest from staff, 'There were no triggers for his behaviour.' But there is always a trigger, a reason, for the response of the pupil on the autistic spectrum. The problem is that we are not always able to identify it. One helpful way forward with this is to have someone act as a 'fly on the wall', carefully observing and listening to identify what may cause the negative reaction.

Consider this example. A Key Stage 2 child was reported to be throwing tantrums, screaming and physically assaulting staff. The adults supporting him were unable to identify the triggers for the behaviour. Following observation things became clearer. On one occasion his visual schedule indicated that the next session was to be ICT in the IT suite, a favoured place and activity. As the rest of the group lined up to leave the room he took his place in the queue. The classroom teacher said, 'Not you, James, you have to finish your science first.' Meltdown occurred, with the full set of behaviours described. Was there a trigger for this behaviour? Of course there was. What was looked forward to and expected was not going to happen. There was no warning of the change. Did James settle down to his science? Absolutely not.

How could the situation have been improved? When James entered the room his visual schedule should have said, 'Science', followed by 'ICT'. The incentive for completing the science is then the reward of his favoured activity. James needed to be warned of what was about to happen. He needed to have a predictable schedule. He could not cope with the sudden change. The trigger was clear, but it took an objective observer to recognize it.

Be proactive to avoid confusion that leads to anxiety and outbursts. Bring in an outside observer if necessary. Ensure that sessions are made predictable through well-planned, visual schedules and consistent management.

READING EXPRESSIONS

Reading facial expression can be a very difficult skill for pupils with autism to master. Our eyes and mouth, the tilt of our head and our posture convey messages that most of us can read very quickly. When we look at a friend we may respond with, 'Are you alright?' or 'You look excited.' How do we know?

The dilemma for pupils with autism is that they often don't know. They are left bewildered by what everyone around them is able to discern. Teaching facial expression and body language is another area that needs to be tackled head on. Although there are software programs and commercial material available, this need can also be met when these resources are not available and it does not have to be an expensive undertaking.

Your face is a wonderful human resource that can be used to effect in helping your pupils to recognize subtle facial expressions. Make faces, have them mirrored by the pupil, have the pupil guess what you are attempting to convey. This can be done in a group and made into a game. Point out expressions on individuals throughout the day. Reassure the pupil that a face that is not smiling does not necessarily indicate a face that is cross or upset. Use faces from magazines, clips from TV soaps where high levels of emotion are depicted and analyse the facial expression and body language. When the emotion is identified, help the pupil to give a reason. Ask, 'Why do you think he looks like that?' Providing understanding of the expressions and posture begins to help raise the awareness of the young person.

As I reflected on something I needed to remember one day, one of my pupils looked troubled and asked, 'Why are you looking like that? Are you angry?' I replied that I was thinking and it was my thinking face. I could also have used the word concentrating. It is useful to give the pupil this type of label to avoid him becoming anxious when a face is not relaxed and smiling.

A common assumption about autism is that people on the spectrum do not make eye contact. While this is true for some individuals, it is not true for all. There can be a range of issues regarding eye contact. Some pupils may avoid looking at others – we know from people with autism who have been able to explain this that it is sometimes because the sensory overload of looking at your face while listening reduces the ability to comprehend what is being said.

Some individuals with poor eye contact have been told so frequently, 'Look at me when I am speaking', that they develop a fixed stare and do not move the focus of their eyes away. This can be very disconcerting.

How do we address these issues? Demonstrate and encourage eye contact to acknowledge others when greeting, and cue the pupil in to look when drawing attention to something. Monitor the situation and be aware that insisting on eye contact may reduce the pupil's ability to respond to other stimuli such as the words you are saying. If staring is a problem, teach a rule about how long we maintain eye contact before blinking or looking away and help the pupil to rehearse this. Remind the pupil regularly when the rules are forgotten and praise him when he achieves success.

THE EYES HAVE IT

A RULE IS A RULE

Many individuals with Asperger's syndrome will find rules a supportive way to work out what is expected day by day. You probably wish sometimes that all your pupils followed the rules to the letter. The difficulty is that we sometimes relax the rules. But rules provide much-needed predictability and help explain how the pupil should perform.

Consider this scenario. There is a rule in the school that pupils have to walk on the left of the corridor. When the teachers are watching this may succeed, but frequently throughout the day the rule is broken. The young person with Asperger's syndrome is walking along the corridor on the left. Others are walking towards him on the right and a collision is inevitable. The group stay on the right but our pupil continues forward on the left because that is what the rule says. Who is in the right? Technically it is our pupil, but by not being flexible an unnecessary confrontation is sparked. A situation such as this demonstrates why the pupil on the autistic spectrum is vulnerable. The inability to respond to the give and take that others assume can lead to tension.

Along with this, the young person on the spectrum may also consider himself the 'rule police' in the school and make sure the teacher knows when anyone has broken a rule. This is not only annoying to members of staff, but makes the pupil a target as peers weary of the constant tale-telling. Finding a way to manage this type of behaviour is important. Establishing a rule with the pupil and delivering it consistently may be helpful. For example, emphasize that the members of staff in the school will enforce the rules. The pupil's role is to make sure he knows and follows the rules. When the pupil reverts to trying to take over, the rule should be repeated in the same way, for example, 'Thank you for pointing that out, but I will deal with it.' This will require staff liaison to ensure that everyone is responding consistently.

How often do we hear this in the classroom and playground? 'It isn't fair!' Children on the spectrum frequently utter these words as they often fail to recognize the perspective of others.

An example may help to clarify this. Martin was in a secondary school class where he and a number of peers were talking. The teacher spoke to some of the others who responded with the typical, 'Sorry, Miss'. When she spoke to Martin he overreacted and hurled verbal abuse at the teacher. She responded by giving him a detention and he then erupted and ran out of the room. In discussion Martin was adamant that it wasn't fair. He had been given a detention and the others hadn't. He only recognized that the crime – talking in class – was the same. It was only after a great deal of examining the situation that Martin began to see why he was the one with the detention. The detention was not for talking, but rather for the abusive language in response.

Give the pupil time to regain composure and then find a way to get to the root of the problem and clarify the issues. Help the pupil to recognize that we all think things that we do not say aloud. We 'bite our tongues' (but remember that if you present it like this the literal interpretation could be a disaster!).

Use these thought and speech bubbles to help the pupil realize the difference between thought and word.

PERSPECTIVE

This term was mentioned in the previous idea but needs to be expanded on. For the most part we are able to see things from the point of view of others. We are able to see what they see and feel. This is another area of difficulty for many people on the autistic spectrum and it can have a huge impact on their ability to cope day by day.

When you are standing in front of a class you know what your pupils see when they look at you and the front of the room. You could describe the scene around and behind you as well as what you see before you. This is very difficult for pupils with autism. Is it any wonder then that they are unable to interpret the emotional perspective of others?

To support development in this area explain how another individual feels when sad, hurt or upset. Connect the language of emotion with the facial expression and behaviour, for example, 'Susan is sad because she fell down' or 'Tom is crying because you kicked him.' If the pupil laughs at another's distress, explain why this is inappropriate and help him to see the reason behind the distress.

I recall with sadness the day one of my pupils asked the classroom assistant how many friends she had. She responded that she had many, too many to count and asked him how many he had. He replied that he had two, thought about it and reduced the number to one and after further pondering he replied, 'No. I don't think so. I don't have any.' For many pupils with autism this is a very difficult part of their lives and one that can cause discouragement and depression.

How do we foster friendship? What makes a friend? For those of us who have wide circles of friends we have probably never given much thought to these questions. We almost 'fall into' friendships and we sustain them across time. How can we support pupils with autism in developing friendships when it just doesn't come naturally?

There is no more distressing situation than when a pupil is always on the outside of the group, always the last one to be picked, the one to eat alone in the cafeteria, the one isolated in the playground. It is our duty to take the responsibility to nurture friendships and to enable relationships to be built in an attempt to reduce the vulnerability of the pupil.

This is another area that has to be nurtured. Find out the pupil's interests and try to pair him with another child who shares the interest. Look for the pupil's strengths and give him an opportunity to support a peer who lacks these strengths. For example, the pupil may be an excellent reader and could read text to a peer who struggles in this way. On the other hand, comprehension is often weaker for the child with autism and may be a strength for the poor decoder, so the support could be mutually beneficial. This can build a bond that can be nurtured outside the classroom.

CHALLENGING BEHAVIOUR

Difficult behaviour is an area of great concern and ultimately is often responsible for the break down of placements within mainstream school. Schools and members of staff vary in how they would describe challenging behaviour and in the tolerance levels with which it is handled. Too often we tend to tar all situations with the same brush and neglect to look at the reasons for the behaviour within the disability of the pupil.

We have become more sensitive in our response to pupils who have other disabilities – a visual or hearing impairment, for example – and respond by making the appropriate allowances for differentiated work and management. We would, for example, be supportive of enlarged print and make allowances for the fact that the visually impaired pupil could not read small font. We certainly wouldn't prevent a pupil from wearing a hearing aid and from sitting at the front of the class. If the pupil needs to see the teacher's face to enable lip-reading, we would take this on board and accommodate the pupil's needs once made aware of them.

How do we respond to a pupil on the autistic spectrum who does not fit the accepted pattern of sitting still, does not follow verbal instructions that are delivered at speed, and does not readily participate within the group? Unfortunately, we often see the child as uninterested, disruptive and uncooperative, rather than recognizing the inherent difficulties related to autism.

What allowances need to be made? Suggestions have been made in other sections, but to summarize:

o Consistent management
o Support, as necessary, from a learning support assistant
o Visual instructions
o Verbal prompts
o Positive use of language
o Specific teaching on how to organize
o Clearly stated instructions, supported by demonstration
o Time to explain expectations
o Planned peer support.

When the response to behaviour is to remove the pupil from the situation, berate him for lack of cooperation and give negative messages, we are missing the point. We are removing the hearing aid or reducing the size of print. Adaptations are essential and must be provided.

MEETING AND GREETING

One of the difficulties in building relationships and establishing friendships can be the aloofness of the pupil. It may appear that he has no interest in or desire for contact with others. Peers may perceive this as snobbery, which certainly doesn't help the pupil to be accepted. Similarly, members of staff do not build up relationships with a pupil who does not acknowledge or respond to them. This indifference on the part of the pupil is not usually a deliberate attempt to ignore, so much as a lack of awareness about the social nature that makes greetings and farewells important.

This is another area that can be addressed directly with the pupil to help him understand what is expected. Without forcing the issue and making it uncomfortable for the pupil, help him to learn to nod or say hello to let others know that he has arrived and is part of the group. Likewise, when leaving a situation, teach the pupil to get the attention of others in the group and to let them know through a wave or a goodbye that he is leaving. It can be helpful to support this by having a greeting sign on the door entering a room and a farewell sign on the opposite side. These visual prompts can then be referred to as a reminder of coming and going behaviour.

This term was drilled into me when I was training to be a teacher. When the opportunity arises to emphasize a skill or concept, capitalize on it! For example, seeing a bee collect nectar from a flower and ignoring it only to teach it a week later in the isolation of the classroom is a lost opportunity.

During each day there are opportunities to teach social skills. Throughout every day the pupil and peers will make social blunders that should be capitalized on rather than ignored. It is these real opportunities that bring the rules of social behaviour to life. If the pupil walks into someone else, stop and explain how to negotiate a busy corridor, how to pause and say excuse me. If the pupil fails to respond when others greet him, explain why this is an important part of letting people know they were heard. If the pupil insults you or a peer, talk it through and make him aware of the way the other person feels. If the pupil misjudges a situation and misinterprets the intentions or demeanour of another, take time to explain what the reality of the situation is.

It is only through taking advantage of the real-life teaching moments that the pupil will begin to recognize the social rules in context.

THE TEACHING MOMENT

Creating the right environment

At times we have all found ourselves in situations where raised voices occur. How do we respond? If it's watching a football match we expect the atmosphere to be loud and we cope well. If it is in a quiet restaurant and voices erupt there is every possibility that all heads will turn and everyone will look at the offenders. We may, in this setting, become anxious, aware of a possible threat to ourselves or even become aggressive in defence of the situation.

Schools do not have to be places where voices are regularly raised and yet they often are. How did it happen that child control became based on aggressively loud adult voices? In the context of the classroom and the school many children do less than their best when the environment is loud. Often, of course, the louder the teacher, the louder the class and the situation escalates throughout the lesson. For many pupils on the autistic spectrum there is a direct correlation between the volume within the room and their inability to focus on the lesson. For many, when a member of staff shouts it is perceived as a direct threat, causing anxiety and possibly raising aggression in defence of the perceived threat.

Atmosphere and ethos are of paramount importance in our schools. Working towards an environment that is supportive through mutual respect and measured response must be a goal we all share. Creating this environment enhances the learning potential for all pupils and enables pupils on the autistic spectrum to *thrive* instead of *cope*. Watch your decibels!

'TAKE OUT YOUR BOOKS.'

'Please take out your books.'

Predictability and routine are crucially important for most people on the autistic spectrum. Surprises are not fun and flexibility can be a nightmare. Throughout the school day and week there are often changes that occur which most pupils take in their stride. There may be a supply teacher, a change of room, a change of time or you may have rearranged the furniture. For many pupils on the autistic spectrum such seemingly minor changes alter their ability to cope with the environment. The response may be one of confusion, rejection or raised anxiety. The heightened anxiety can then spill over into difficult behaviour. Very often, staff and peers are left shaking their heads wondering what has gone wrong.

What has gone wrong? Something has changed. Things are not the way they are meant to be and this has created fear and uncertainty. What can you do to reduce these reactions and provide security?

o Warn of change wherever possible.
o Explain why the change is going to occur.
o Emphasize the things that are consistent about the day.
o Be prepared for the reaction and offer security.

We cannot prevent change. We cannot stop things from moving on. But we can be aware of the anxiety it creates, be sensitive to the situation and attempt to minimize the disruption.

A PREDICTABLE ROUTINE

MAKE IT VISUAL

Many of us are visual learners, perhaps more than we realize. We keep a diary and we refer to it to remind us of what is ahead of us at the beginning of the day. We follow road signs to be guided along a journey that we would not be able to negotiate purely by memory. We write 'to do' lists to keep us on task. And yet, we often fail to recognize how oral and non-visual we are in working with children.

Here's an example. The lesson begins and the teacher says, 'Open your books, turn to page 53 and do questions one to six. When you have finished put your books on the corner of my desk and get on with your diagram.' The pupils in the group who are ready to listen before the instruction began and who pick up instructions quickly are now almost ready to get on with the task. However, the pupil on the autistic spectrum who struggles with language processing and who is still back at 'Open your . . .' is completely unable to get on with the task. Finding it difficult to ask for your help (possibly assuming that the teacher expects him to know without being asked), the pupil fails to begin the work and may then be reprimanded and the situation begins to escalate.

Reinforce the oral instruction with a quick written instruction:

> Find page 53 in your book
> Do questions one to six
> Put finished books on my desk
> Draw diagram

Spoken words disappear into the ether while visual instructions can be referred to as often as required.

Some pupils with autism are able to cope with the type of visual presentation described in Idea 35. For others, a much more detailed approach is required. A visual timetable prepares the entire day for the child, building in the necessary predictability and routine. The timetable uses motivators (things the pupil likes the most) to follow tasks that may not be favoured. The presentation of the timetable should be based on individual need. It can be presented in photographic or symbol form or it may be presented in words. As the needs of the child change, so will the way in which the timetable is organized. For example:

Laminating the symbols and displaying them on a Velcro strip makes the job manageable and allows you to demonstrate change when necessary. Bearing in mind that the schedule will change every day and that there will be unaccounted for changes that may create anxiety, this flexibility is essential to success.

As the pupil becomes able to process written language the timetable may be presented as:

Reading
Art
Writing
Computer   (favoured activity)
Lunch
Geography
Music
Trains   (favoured activity)
Home

In secondary school the timetable is often part of the diary provided by the school. In this way the pupil will not stand out from peers. However, it may be necessary to colour code the subjects and accompany the timetable with a colour-coded map to help the pupil to find his way around school. The important thing to bear in mind is the need to match the timetable to the understanding of the pupil.

CUE CARDS

Many of us have developed systems to cue ourselves in to remember information. A system of cue cards – visual cards about the size of a credit card that clearly outline information – to support pupils on the autistic spectrum can be a useful aid to recall and to independence. The best way to demonstrate this is through practical examples.

I will try to remember to bring:
- pencil
- pen
- rubber
- ruler
- the right book

To every lesson.

When I do not understand I will ask a member of staff for help.

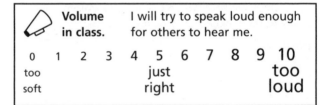

	Volume in class.	I will try to speak loud enough for others to hear me.

0	1	2	3	4	5	6	7	8	9	10
too soft					just right					too loud

The cue cards are visual; they use clear text and are available for the pupil in all lessons. They may be laminated and carried in the pupil's pocket or diary. The cards must be specific to the individual need, and developed *with the pupil*, ensuring that all terms are fully understood.

Many individuals on the autistic spectrum struggle within the environment, having sensitivities to sound, touch, sight, smell and taste. This can make everyday situations overwhelmingly difficult to contend with. Concentration and learning can be blocked and behaviour can be affected.

SOUND

We tend to block out many sounds in the environment and get on with life in spite of them. For some of your pupils this may not be possible. For example, the humming of a fluorescent light, the ringing of the telephone in an office, the barking of a dog in a nearby garden, the noise of peers playing outside or in the sports hall, could all affect a pupil. You may not hear the sounds, while at the same time they are proving to be a distraction or perhaps even a cause of anxiety for the pupil.

TOUCH

For most of us brushing against someone in the corridor is no big deal; touching a range of pieces of equipment, wearing a uniform or carrying a bag over our shoulder are all taken in our stride. Not so for the individual who is hypersensitive to touching and being touched. Labels may have to be removed from clothing, new clothing may have to be washed several times before it is soft enough to wear, or a particular grip may be necessary on a pen or pencil.

SIGHT

Lighting can be a distraction, particularly the flickering of a fluorescent bulb that causes the pupil to want to shut the light out. When we see a pupil with his eyes closed we usually think boredom, but this may not be the case. We deliberately provide a stimulating environment with bright colours and patterns. Many individuals on the spectrum describe the pain they experience when a patterned carpet overwhelms their space or a bright colour seems to move in on them.

SENSORY OVERLOAD

SMELL AND TASTE

These areas will have a particular impact at meal times and in food technology. The aroma coming from the school kitchen may overwhelm the senses if the lesson before lunch is in a nearby classroom. The odour and tactile nature of foods being prepared by the pupil may cause distress. There are often issues related to diet and what the pupil will eat. In addition to this he may have an overtly negative response to body odour (good and bad) and react to the person emitting the odour.

How can sensory issues be addressed?

○ Ensure that staff are alert to the sensory triggers that may cause anxiety.
○ Support the pupil by reassuring and explaining what is causing the overload.
○ Modify lighting, where possible, to reduce fluorescent flicker.
○ Allow the pupil to be seated in a low distraction area, not surrounded by over-stimulating colour and display.
○ When redecorating, consider calm colours that soothe.
○ Ensure that adequate dinner options are available.
○ Create a calm, quiet atmosphere throughout the school.

Life takes on a whole new dimension when a pupil moves from primary to secondary school. Let's think about some of the changes. In primary school the pupils are, for the most part, in one classroom with one teacher delivering the curriculum. There are usually integrated cloakrooms, making it easy to keep things together. There are trays with nicely labelled names for the pupils to know where to put their exercise books and equipment. Then, almost without warning, comes the local comprehensive secondary school.

One of the first things on the agenda for many pupils, and certainly for pupils on the autistic spectrum, should be a series of induction sessions on organization. What would this entail?

○ Colour-coded books and timetable to ensure the pupil has the right things for the right lesson. In some schools this coincides with colour-coded floors or corridors for pupils to find their way around the building.
○ Labelling equipment to ensure it remains the property of the pupil.
○ A clearly presented map showing the layout of all the school.
○ Clear explanations of the school rules, translated into positive, user-friendly language that is understood.
○ Photographs of staff supporting the child, names and curriculum areas.
○ Information about the etiquette of changing for PE.
○ Information on the dining room, options related to dinner and how to navigate the system.
○ Awareness-raising of who to go to for help when things go wrong.
○ Information on how to stay safe and avoid being vulnerable.

If the time is taken to lay the foundation it is so much more likely that the pupil will not come tumbling down.

LET'S GET ORGANIZED

IDEA

40

A SAFE HAVEN

Most children thrive on the fun times and drag their heels when it is time to return to class. Not so for pupils on the autistic spectrum. It is the routine, managed and predictable parts of the day that they cope with best and the non-structured times that create anxiety and uncertainty. There may be an easy answer to this that is too often overlooked by schools. This is to find a safe place where pupils can go when they are uncertain or uncomfortable with the environment. What will this safe haven look like? It may be:

○ the library, open for use during breaks and dinner times
○ a room set aside for board games or quiet reflection and relaxation
○ a quiet area near the SENCO's office
○ a classroom where a teacher is happy to welcome one or two pupils just to come in and 'chill'
○ an opportunity to have some responsibility and help a member of staff.

One size does not fit all. The important thing to remember is that for some pupils the 'fun' times are torture and create such anxiety that difficult behaviour escalates and the lessons that follow are unnecessarily fractious. So, consider the pupil's needs and find a safe haven.

In contrast to peers who can hardly wait for lessons to end and breaks to begin, one of the most difficult times for pupils with autism is when the structure is reduced. Before and after school, breaks, ends of lessons, walking in the corridor, going for the bus, are all times when vulnerability is raised. When you rely heavily on structure and schedules to see you through the day and those props are withdrawn, is it any wonder that anxiety increases?

One girl I worked with described playtime for me. She said, 'I walk slowly around the playground and hope no one notices me.' This is a not uncommon picture of a pupil with autism – walking alone on the perimeter of play and socialization. With limited social skills it is very difficult to break into the group and when your advances are out of the ordinary you can become further rejected and isolated.

To support unstructured times, direct the pupil to an activity and encourage an appropriate group of peers to engage with the pupil. Consider whether it is necessary for the pupil to be with the crowd and monitor the situation to reduce vulnerability. Provide opportunities for the pupil to do some jobs in the classroom rather than leave this safe environment, or allocate a safe place in the dining room where supervision is available. Allow the pupil to walk the corridor slightly before the end of lessons. If a support assistant is assigned to the pupil, schedule the assistant's time across unstructured parts of the day, with a focus on developing social skills and facilitating peer relationships.

WHOLE-SCHOOL UNDERSTANDING

At the very heart of success of working with pupils on the autistic spectrum is the necessity for whole-school understanding. As much as some dedicated members of staff may seek to create the right environment, the entire day is fraught with potential pitfalls and misunderstandings. Unless there is a shared understanding and commitment, the pupil will experience inconsistent management and mixed messages that will prevent coping and inhibit learning.

To achieve this whole-school understanding it is essential that staff training is a priority. The difficulty will always remain that training in one disability area is competing for other priorities in the school calendar. However, reflecting on what was said in Idea 1, the lessons we learn are 'good practice for all', therefore not competing with but complementing the needs of all pupils throughout the school.

Many authorities have a dedicated team of advisory teachers to support staff working with children with autism. There are many opportunities for 'bespoke' training to address the individual needs of the pupils in a school and to provide individualized strategies and interventions to support needs.

The SENCO and inclusion coordinator need to make ASD training a priority on the school agenda. There should be organized twilight sessions for key members of staff and if possible, you should participate in authority-wide training. And remember to seek support regularly from ASD advisory staff. It is time that training becomes the right of the pupil rather than an optional extra.

Recent statistics show that more than 25 per cent of pupils on the autistic spectrum have been excluded from our schools. It would be difficult to argue that autism is accepted as a disability that educational establishments are willing to cope with. This doesn't simply have an effect on the pupil, but goes to the heart of what parents struggle with when they have a child with autism – a lack of acceptance.

How do we begin to turn this around and find ways to accept a different kind of 'normal'? When did we begin to believe that all our pupils should be able to respond in like manner to the daily rigours of school and society?

At the heart of acceptance is understanding and this can only be achieved through training that includes every member of the school community. Keep autism on the agenda to encourage ongoing understanding and acceptance through whole-staff awareness-raising, along with in-depth training for SENCOs and key members of SEN staff. Where there are behaviour managers within the school, it will be necessary for them to develop an understanding of the difference between the management of pupils with ASD and other behavioural difficulties that they manage. Part of the information-sharing should include regular updates in the staffroom, at briefings or in the school bulletin.

As staff awareness is improved it will be easier to recognize the need for adaptations to the environment and greater tolerance of difference will be established. It is only when we seek to change the climate of sameness that we will begin to have an attitude of acceptance.

AN ATTITUDE OF ACCEPTANCE

MESSAGES HOME

Home–school communication is an important aspect of making school a success for pupils on the autistic spectrum. The danger is that very often the communication is negative, reporting what the child has done wrong or failed to do at all. As with the rest of us, it is always best to start with the positive and turn the negative into how improvement can be made. Devise a simple way of communicating with the parents – a sheet that can be filled in at the end of the day will be enough. For example:

👍	What went well today?
❓	What can be improved?
🎯	Target for tomorrow:

In this way the pupil and parents are receiving a positive, realistic picture of the day, but the focus is also on how to improve. This may be a daily or weekly system based on the needs of the pupil. It should be produced *with* the pupil to give him ownership of both the successes and the areas for development.

By engaging in home–school communication there is a better opportunity for consistency and the pupil recognizes that school and home are integrated, breaking down the barriers of the home–school divide.

For pupils on the autistic spectrum one of the most challenging parts of the school week can be assembly. Very often the environment is overwhelming, with large numbers of bodies in a reverberating room. The sensory issues, as discussed in Idea 38, can create total discomfort for the pupil.

These difficulties can be especially challenging in a primary school when the children are often seated on the floor and assembly is held in the same room that is used for dinner, with lingering odours from the kitchen. If acoustics are a problem the pupil may make noises to hear the echo within the room.

Some small adaptations can benefit the pupil's ability to cope:

o Ensure that assembly is on the visual timetable.
o Seat the pupil at the end of the row where there is less physical contact with other children.
o Recognize the sensory difficulties and allow the pupil to leave if these become overwhelming.
o Provide visual prompts to encourage the pupil to be quiet and face the front of the room.

Give careful consideration to how much the pupil is benefiting from attending assembly and whether or not this time would be better spent providing some of the discrete teaching time that is mentioned throughout the book.

DO I HAVE TO GO TO ASSEMBLY?

CREATIVITY

If I could choose one quality as paramount for staff who support the needs of pupils on the autistic spectrum to have it would be creativity. Within this one feature lies the essence of how to be successful. Individuals with creativity do not give up at the first hurdle because they can always find another way forward. They don't abandon an idea because it didn't work, they 'tweak' it to make it more successful. They look at a problem and through analysing it they develop a solution. Hence, there is the potential for success.

Can creativity be taught or is it a gift? That is a difficult question to answer, but we will approach it as if you can cultivate the skill by taking the time to get to know the pupil, recognizing strengths and tapping into them. Throughout sessions, watch for reactions and behaviours that fit into the triad of impairments for autism – communication, socialization and resistance to change. Reflect on what you see and try to find possible solutions. When an idea fails, be persistent in seeking further information from published material or colleagues, and refuse to give up when others would.

A pupil on the autistic spectrum who is supported by individuals with creativity will have opportunities to meet with success.

It is not unusual for pupils in secondary school to be 'set' in ability groups. Frequently, this results in lower ability groups overlapping with pupils who are disaffected by school and challenge the teacher to teach. Although many pupils with Asperger's syndrome will have average or above intelligence, their pattern of learning may be such that they have not achieved well and as a consequence they too frequently end up in lower sets.

The ethos and environment of the group may make the pupil feel vulnerable, resulting in raised anxiety and what then appears to be lack of cooperation. I would argue that the best place for a pupil on the autistic spectrum is in a class group where management is strong and the environment is conducive to learning. In this context the pupil is more relaxed, confident, and more able to access the curriculum. If the work is a challenge the teacher has more opportunity to support the pupil because others in the group are able to manage much of their own learning. If there is a learning support assistant with the pupil, he/she can work across the group, enabling the teacher to spend more time teaching and moving the ASD pupil and others along.

It is breaking with tradition to accommodate a pupil who has not reached a certain standard in an upper set, but you will not know what the ASD pupil is capable of if the environment is not appropriate.

SETTING

WHO CAN HELP?

When supporting a pupil on the autistic spectrum it is not uncommon for the key individual to feel isolated. Autism is a complex condition, with each pupil having a unique presentation of needs. Various professionals should be available to help untangle the dilemmas that are presented to support staff within the school. A whole-school understanding is paramount and within this the keyworker should be able to rely on:

o a sensitive management team
o a well-informed SENCO
o colleagues experienced in SEN
o an educational psychologist
o a speech and language therapist
o an ASD advisory teacher
o Child and Adolescent Mental Health Service team members
o parents/carers.

It may take some ingenuity to draw the professionals together to discuss the issues and develop an action plan to address needs. Persevere in this, articulating the right of the pupil to be supported by a multi-disciplinary team and recognizing that sharing experience and good practice can help in problem solving. Within this, do not overlook the valuable contribution of the pupil's parents/carers who have known him longer than any professionals and may have insight into behaviours and frustrations that you fail to see. We need to respect them as a resource for understanding and recognize that they are essential in addressing the issues of consistency that are so important to the pupil's well-being.

Coping strategies

Homework is one of the most challenging areas for many pupils on the autistic spectrum. Often the two worlds of home and school are separated to the degree that the pupil does not want to associate them. This is one of the reasons why home–school liaison is so important.

Some schools attempt to support pupils by having a homework club at dinnertime or after school. But remember the issues of literal understanding (see Idea 18)? It's *home*work we're talking about, making it very difficult for the pupil to accept that it can be done at school.

Often, when the work goes home it becomes a matter of great anxiety and as parents attempt to help they are met with the 'you're not my teacher' attitude and perceived as not having the skills to support when help is needed. Many parents report distress and aggression when homework is tackled in the evenings. If staff are aware of these conflicts they can help to reduce them by using their 'professional' voice to encourage the pupil to ask the parent for help and to affirm that staff and parents work together. By doing this you are, in a way, giving the 'licence' to the parents and helping the pupil to accept their parents' support as valid.

How else can you reduce this anxiety and help the pupil to accept a flexible approach? Clearly explain what homework is and why it is important. Identify the start and finish point of the assignment and demonstrate how much time should be spent on the homework. Praise the pupil when work is completed successfully. To avoid confusion, use visual cues (see Idea 37) to explain about homework clubs. For example:

Teachers give homework to help you learn more about what you are studying at school. It can be done at home or in the homework club during the dinner break. If you finish your work in the club you do not have to take it home to do. If you do your work at the club there is a member of staff to help you. When you work at home your parents can help you with your work. Teachers are happy for parents to help.

Another cause of anxiety for a pupil with autism can be associated with supply teachers. The need for sameness, routine and predictability means that facing a new person at the front of the class or as support brings confusion and uncertainty. The pupil needs to be helped to cope with such change.

Whenever possible warn the pupil in advance that the member of staff will be absent. However, this is not always feasible – if a teacher is ill – and it is important that the pupil is prepared for the unplanned change. A useful strategy is to write a Social Story™ (see Idea 51), explaining that there are times when a member of staff cannot be at school. The story should emphasize what will be consistent when this one change occurs; for example, the room, peers, other staff, curriculum area, exercise books, will remain constant.

We all know that in some instances the nature of the lesson changes dramatically when the regular member of staff is absent. If the situation results in the pupil being vulnerable and becoming anxious, there is a risk that he will be totally unable to cope. In that case, withdrawal from the lesson should be considered. This should, however, be a last resort as learning to cope with change is essential to future development.

SUPPLY STAFF

IDEA

51

SOCIAL STORIES™

Social Stories™ is a strategy developed by Carol Gray and used widely to support social understanding for pupils on the autistic spectrum. You will not become an expert by reading this description and would benefit from finding a course where Social Stories™ are explained in detail.

When a pupil is struggling to grasp an issue, this strategy can offer a clear and consistent approach to improve understanding. One of the underlying features is the clarity with which the story is written, the positive and affirming style and the total consistency with which the story is then delivered to the pupil. The story should take account of several factors in relation to the pupil:

○ Age
○ Reading and comprehension
○ Attention span
○ Interests
○ Preferred learning style.

It is not a quick fix and requires regular rehearsal to embed the principles in the pupil's mind. Carol Gray has found her Social Stories™ a positive approach over many years and through sharing this strategy with professionals all over the world she has enabled many individuals with autism to cope with change and increase flexibility.

We often think of transition with respect to moving from one Key Stage to another or one school to another. In fact, transition occurs throughout each day. Coming to school, moving from room to room, activity to activity and going home again are all transition points. When change is difficult this results in numerous times throughout the day when anxiety is raised and the potential for struggling to cope is heightened.

Our role is to plan for transition and reduce anxiety. To do this it is important to ensure that the pupil knows what is happening next and where (refer to visual timetables, Idea 36). But this in itself is not sufficient; the anxiety is due in part to negotiating the journey from room to room. The school bell may cause sensory overload, the crowded nature of the corridor and jostling for position in a queue adds to the situation, the insecurity about having the right equipment creates further uncertainty and the whole process becomes an escalating trauma for the young person.

Try to be flexible and allow the pupil to leave the lesson slightly before the group and walk along a quiet corridor. Engage peers to offer support during such times. Be alert and sensitive to the heightened apprehensions when the pupil begins the new session. These are the keys to reducing anxiety and enabling the pupil to cope as he goes through the day.

TAP INTO PEERS

Too often young people on the autistic spectrum are left to cope in a peer-dominated environment without the understanding or support of other pupils. While we have to be sensitive to the disclosure of a label without the consent of the young person, if we are able to help the peer group understand why the pupil reacts as he does we are more likely to have their cooperation.

Identify a group of peers who have qualities that lend themselves to empathy and concern for others. Once identified, help them to understand the nature of the difficulties and ask them to 'keep an eye out', to walk with and reassure the pupil with autism, thereby contributing to the success of school life. We don't use this valuable resource enough. The benefits are twofold – it gives the pupil with autism a sense of support and it fosters empathy among peers and thus prepares them for future roles in society.

Through peer support we are also providing role models and helping the autistic pupil to recognize the role of others in his life. This in turn helps to enable him to cope in an otherwise potentially frightening environment.

While whole-school understanding is the goal for supporting pupils on the autistic spectrum, it will be impossible for every individual member of staff to have a full and complete picture of the individual pupil. There will inevitably be some who know and understand the pupil better and who will be the key to success.

The role of the SENCO cannot be underestimated, as this person is responsible for pupils with SEN and for cascading information to other staff. The recruitment and appointment of learning support assistants will fall to the SENCO, and this process of ensuring that the right people are selected and that training is provided will have long-term impact on the pupil and the school. It is often the learning support assistant who develops the strongest relationship with the pupil with autism and who begins to recognize the individual needs and unique personality.

Learning mentors are now part of many staff teams and contribute to the support of individual pupils who struggle with fitting into the routine of daily school life. If they are to take autism 'under their wing' they *must* be trained to recognize the difference in the way these pupils see and respond to the world.

Whole-school understanding involves the caretaker, lunchtime organizers and administration staff who will come into regular contact with the pupil. It is so easy for the pattern of consistent management to break down if we fail to ensure we have passed relevant information to all adults in the school. To this end the SENCO should take the responsibility to provide a system of 'in-house' training that includes these adults. This should provide concise written information for discussion and reference. When new members of staff join the school, part of their induction should be to learn about ASD in general and individual pupils in particular.

When awareness is raised it is not unusual for a member of staff we would have possibly overlooked to become a champion for the pupil.

ADULT MENTORS

Why do we work? Let's be honest now. I have a suspicion that it is highly aligned with the incentive at the end of the month. And yet we expect our pupils to work for lengthy periods of time with no tangible recognition of what they are doing. Motivation is often lacking in pupils with autism. This may be because they do not see the reason for the task. If they know the work already it will be difficult to motivate pupils to do work for work's sake. They may struggle to see the point of writing the answers down if they know them internally. So, how do we help to motivate?

One very positive way to encourage the pupil to do his work or finish a task once started is to provide an incentive. It is often successful to build this on a 'First . . . then . . .' approach. Consider these examples:

> *First finish your writing, and then you may finish the drawing.*
> *First read the passage, then you can look at your book.*
> *First write up the experiment, and then it will be time for break.*

The 'then . . .' is the motivator and what works best will change with each pupil. For a primary school pupil it may be work first, then trains, or numbers first, then water play. At secondary school, if the pupil has a special interest (very common) use this as an incentive. The pupil could have a file with information, drawing paper or books on the special interest. Keep the file back until the task has been completed. Like us, children and young people often need the reward at the end of the month. Let's not make decisions that deter the pupil from being motivated to learn.

DEALING WITH STRESS

Stress and anxiety figure frequently throughout the ideas in this book. For many reasons the individual with autism often experiences anxiety and stress and if not addressed appropriately this can lead to anger and aggression. Knowing this makes it essential that those supporting the pupil try to help him recognize the signs of stress and develop coping strategies that prevent 'meltdown'.

This is best dealt with in discrete sessions with the pupil or a small group of pupils where the physical symptoms of stress are explained. I once worked with a pupil who thought he was having a heart attack because he could feel his heart beating when he was upset. Detailing the changes in our bodies when we are anxious helps the pupil to understand the symptoms but also to recognize when he needs help or to move away from a situation. Try using a diagram of the body with labels to identify flushed cheeks, sweaty palms, racing heart, pulse rate, facial expression, upset stomach and so on – this will help the pupil to identify how his body responds to anxiety.

Role-play and drama can be very supportive in showing pupils situations where things have gone wrong and how to respond in a different, more positive way.

One young man I taught had a violent temper that all too frequently led to aggression. Following all incidents we gave him a set time to calm down before letting him explain, as best he could, what had happened. The next question was, 'What did you do?' and this was followed by, 'How else could you have handled the situation?' Before too long this pupil began to monitor his own stress levels and when he knew he was about to blow he would signal that he wanted to go to the toilet. The purpose of this was to put cold water on his face, have some time away from the situation and when he was ready, return to the group. He was, of course, praised for handling the situation well.

We almost always recognize when a pupil has mishandled a situation. We must try to be as rigorous in seeing the many times when the pupil has navigated the problems without incident, and praise him for this.

TIME TO TALK

At the heart of many ideas for developing the pupil's understanding and ability to cope lies the opportunity to spend time with him to address specific issues that are causing anxiety. There are a number of things to bear in mind to make this a success:

○ Make sure a familiar adult with whom the pupil has an established relationship is present.
○ Consider the best time for sessions – for example, the start of the school day, following an incident, at the end of the day.
○ Choose a quiet, comfortable environment that is familiar to the pupil.
○ Use the mode of communication that best suits the pupil.
○ Use a range of visual supports, including scribing for the pupil if appropriate.
○ Allow time for the pupil to articulate the issues.
○ Help the pupil to come up with coping strategies if this is possible.
○ Suggest some ways to help the pupil cope – for example, a cue card to ask to leave a situation, deep breathing, clenching fists in pockets, use of a stress ball.
○ Reassure and praise the pupil when he has coped well.
○ Use a range of approaches, such as role-play, social games, familiar scenarios.

Providing an opportunity for the pupil to explain what he finds difficult to cope with and showing that you are willing to help him find solutions will augur well for his future development.

In the longer term our goal for all our pupils is for them to become independent. This is a necessary stage of development for pupils with autism and by the very nature of their difficulties it is easy for us to increase their dependency on our support. Some of these suggestions may enable you to promote greater independence in pupils:

○ Encourage the pupil to manage his own visual timetable.
○ Break tasks into small, manageable sections to be done independently.
○ Help the pupil to develop personal understanding of his preferred learning environment.
○ Provide technology to support recording and communication.
○ Develop confidence for self-advocacy.
○ Help the pupil to write down and rehearse ideas to express in groups.
○ Provide post-it notes or a mini-whiteboard to record information and write reminders.
○ Provide opportunities for the pupil to take messages to another part of the building, initially when the corridor is empty, but building up to busier times.

Consider throughout each day where you can withdraw and allow the pupil to take charge of his learning and communication.

DEVELOPING INDEPENDENCE

SELF-HELP SKILLS

It is not uncommon for pupils with ASD to have little interest in the fashion trends and normal need for conformity of their peers. Additionally, there may be a lack of awareness with respect to hygiene and appearance. Some of these issues are refreshing and to encourage getting caught up in fashion and trends would be wrong. On the other hand, some require support to reduce the vulnerability of the pupil and to help them develop awareness.

Whatever the problem, ensure that it is addressed sensitively but candidly. For example, if the pupil has body odour a general comment such as, 'Someone doesn't smell very nice' is not going to help. The pupil will have to be informed of why we have body odour and how we eliminate it. Such topics should be done in close collaboration with home and it is sometimes useful to involve a school nurse to 'make it official'.

Dressing can continue to be a problem across the years and may need a specific focus to develop independently. This may involve visual prompts for the sequence of dressing. It is often helpful if the pupil learns to put clothing in an orderly pile when changing for PE, and it may be necessary to explain the phrase 'inside out'.

The school uniform may be worn with precision or it may be dishevelled. If the latter is the case, showing good models and reinforcing the rules in a positive way may be helpful.

Be clear and consistent when pointing out where the pupil is getting it wrong, remembering to demonstrate how to improve.

During our busy daily lives we are often so concerned about *doing* that we do not have time to take a step back and see what is happening around the pupil. If we pause for reflection, we have a sense of guilt that we are not fulfilling our support role. I urge you to find time to observe the pupil and feel confident that through observation you will raise your own awareness of the challenges the pupil faces.

To achieve this you will need to ensure that other staff within the setting are aware of what you are planning to do. Inform the pupil that you will be watching the class for the session and that you must not be interrupted. It is important that the emphasis is on the class rather than the individual in order to maintain, as far as possible, a natural response. Be prepared with pen and paper to take detailed notes.

Watch the pupil and note activity, time on task, concentration, distractions, restlessness, times out of seat, interaction with peers, interaction with adults and response to instruction. Along with this, be sensitive to sound, light, motion, odours and other sensory issues that may make the pupil uncomfortable.

Reflect on the observation and the situation and from this consider whether you are able to improve the learning circumstances for the pupil. Use the information to inform colleagues and to heighten your own awareness of the pupil's needs. If you identify something that you feel is inhibiting the pupil's ability to concentrate or participate, find a way to address this with the pupil and work together to come up with a solution.

OBSERVE TO LEARN

FEEDBACK

When work is marked away from the pupil it is common for errors to be indicated with an X. This is not going to be sufficient for the pupil with autism. Neither is the verbal reprimand of 'Not like that' going to help the pupil to improve performance in the future. In order to aid further understanding, the pupil needs to understand where he went wrong and how to change the error. Check that he has clearly understood the instructions before the work begins. This can be achieved by explaining the error, then modelling the correct method. Always provide a balance of the negative and positive in your feedback.

A common frustration for some pupils with ASD is the untidiness that results from crossing out errors or rubbing a hole in the paper. In such a case the pupil will need to be shown how to score out an error neatly and to accept that this is alright. It may be helpful to show the pupil the work of a peer where this has been done.

Feedback needs to be positive while addressing the incorrect work and explaining how to make the necessary improvements.

Establishing foundations for learning

IDENTIFY STRENGTHS

We too often get caught up in a deficit style of assessing pupils' needs. Individuals on the autistic spectrum have many strengths and when we begin to recognize these we are able to use them to advantage.

While some find it very difficult to be organized, others thrive on organization in minute detail. This is the pupil that can be used to help with classroom organization – 'a place for everything and everything in its place'. One pupil I was observing could not help but tidy all the equipment away at the end of a session and the teacher found this annoying. Let's celebrate such a need and put it to good use while praising the pupil for the role he takes within the group.

For others, strengths may be seen in the curriculum. This may be a special ability in mathematics that will lead to future exam success. Skills may be strong in ICT and this can then be used as a way to seek out other information and present work. It may be a passionate interest in a subject area such as transport or fungi. While it would not be possible to build the whole curriculum around such topics of interest, it is possible to give the pupil the limelight when the passion overlaps with the curriculum, and the special interest can be used as a motivator to encourage completion of other assignments. There may be talent for learning facts and figures that will allow for positive contributions to group projects.

In short, assess the pupil's strengths and praise what he does well. Where possible, use the special interest as a motivator and seek to broaden the topic – for example, a fascination with transport may lead to a study of the development of trains.

A great deal of time has been spent in recent years training teachers to recognize the range of teaching and learning styles represented by the children they teach. Many of you will have identified your own styles and know that they vary considerably. For many people on the autistic spectrum the preferred style is visual and their opportunities for success are increased when information is provided in this way. Teaching often relies on giving a verbal instruction and expecting the pupils to 'get on with it'.

Some examples may clarify this. In a history lesson a pupil may be asked to imagine what it would be like to live in Roman times and to write a story about an evening in the village. Or in an art lesson the pupils are asked to imagine a vase and draw it prior to sculpting it in clay. For a young person on the spectrum the chances of success are minimal. The lack of imagination inhibits the ability to respond to these instructions. To address this issue:

○ provide a photograph or picture to inspire the pupil's writing and ideas
○ use concrete objects to provide a sensory experience
○ write down the instructions so that they can be referred to as needed
○ provide 'here is one I made earlier' models
○ work alongside the pupil to get him started.

When generalization is an area of difficulty it follows that we must work to support the child in making the links between topics and seeing how they can fit together. A very helpful way to link and expand ideas is through mind-maps. This technique provides a clear, visual prompt that supports vocabulary development, connects thoughts and helps to organize writing.

The process of mind-mapping is as important, if not more, than the product. This means that the pupil must be engaged in the development of the map, not just given one that has previously been produced. This example shows how the process works. The new topic introduced to the pupil is paper. Thoughts and words are collected from the pupil, with prompts as necessary, to build onto the map. This can be done in words or pictures if this is more appropriate.

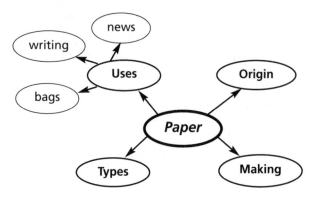

. . . and so on. As the map builds, the vocabulary develops, the links are expanded and the opportunities for research and writing are provided. Throughout the topic the pupil can continue to add new links and refer to the information as needed to keep focused. It is visual (that term again!). It is user friendly and accessible. It is also a very satisfying technique that can be used in any context, be it academic or social.

One of the difficulties faced by the pupil on the autistic spectrum is the confusion of open-ended tasks. Success is more easily achieved when there is a clear start and finish. One pupil, when asked to write as many opposites as he could for homework, worked into the night. His parents could not convince him that he had done enough as the teacher had said, 'As many as you can'. If the teacher had said, 'As many as you can in 30 minutes' or had given a guideline such as, 'Write 20 to 30 opposites', the problem would not have arisen.

This illustration demonstrates, again, the way the child with ASD can be disadvantaged through literal understanding. Consider some of these ideas to support clarity:

○ Give a time limit to a task.
○ Use a highlighter to illustrate which parts of a worksheet require completion.
○ Score off parts of a sheet that are not required.
○ Cover unnecessary information with a post-it note.
○ Write the instructions down to remove any confusion if information is forgotten.
○ Clearly indicate where to write the information and when/where to stop writing.

Such adaptations are not time consuming or in conflict with the needs of others, but can go a long way to support a pupil whose success is impeded by confusion.

CLARITY PLEASE

DIFFERENTIATION

Differentiation has become a common term in schools and for some it seems to be a dreaded word. It emphasizes the point that all pupils do not respond in the same way, do not cope with the same presentation of materials or the same quantity of work. Unfortunately, there are still many times when we seem to expect that an attitude of 'all things to all pupils' will be just fine. Not so.

When we accept that a range of needs is represented in a group it is negligent to ignore the differences. Good practice would suggest that we offer a menu of options such as:

o Enlarged print
o Pen or pencil choice
o Rearrangement of data on a page
o Different methods of recording
o A diagram provided rather than having to draw it
o A varied amount of time to complete the task
o Prompts to keep on task
o Fewer questions for some pupils
o Pupils paired with a peer for support
o Visual or written instructions.

There is a theme running through this book – make it visual! This is crucially important as we consider making the curriculum accessible for pupils with autism. It includes the previously discussed ideas about instructions and schedules, but it doesn't stop there.

Teaching in the twenty-first century enables, through the use of technology, every opportunity to stimulate and support pupils visually. Interactive whiteboards have replaced 'chalk and talk' and, when used to advantage, make it possible for pupils to *see* what the teacher is *saying*. For example, introduce a new era in history or a country in geography through video clips and photographs to bring the topic to life and help to compensate for difficulties with imagining. Pupils can and should be involved in interacting through the wealth of software available across the curriculum. The lesson can begin with display prompts on the board as the pupils enter the room, reminding them of expectations. A slide show of the group working purposefully and the development of a project over time can help maintain interest and provide a backdrop to the lesson. And don't forget that cartoon depiction can bring humour to rules.

By making the most of what is available we not only support the curriculum but also engage the pupil and create a more conducive environment for learning. As emphasized in Idea 1, this is good practice for all.

I NEED TO SEE IT

CURRICULUM-SPECIFIC LANGUAGE

Many pupils on the autistic spectrum will struggle to learn incidentally and to generalize what they have learned. In addition to the impact this has on social behaviour, awareness of the environment and general knowledge, it also has an impact on vocabulary development. Therefore, the pupil's knowledge of terms associated with different subjects in the curriculum may be limited and these will need discrete teaching. When one word has two meanings confusion may occur. If the pupil interprets what you say literally and cannot decipher meaning through context, your message may be lost.

To support understanding consider introducing new vocabulary at the beginning of a new topic to develop a useful word bank. Along with this, introduce subject-specific language, for example, the meaning of compass in mathematics in comparison to geography and orienteering. Demonstrate how the meaning of a word may change in a different curriculum area – 'ruler' in mathematics and 'ruler' in history. Take opportunities to explain these kind of words (homonyms) and build a bank of these to help the pupil recognize them when they occur.

At the heart of many of the difficulties experienced by the pupil with autism is the lack of ability to sort through peripheral information and identify the main idea. Often the stimulus of the environment and the sensory input combine to distract from the real focus. Consider this situation. Mark comes into the classroom and his attention is drawn by the sunlight streaming through the window, the dust particles visible in the air, the scrap of paper on the window ledge and the open window. He totally misses the selection of artefacts on the desks that the peer group has been drawn to. The others in the group know immediately that this lesson is going to follow on from the new topic of archaeology that the teacher introduced in the last lesson. Mark has not noticed. Mark is fascinated by the dust particles in the air.

Similarly when a country is being studied, Mark may be very difficult to engage in its location, political background and economy, but he may be able to tell you every known fact about its flag.

How will you help Mark get the main idea? How will you draw his attention to the focus of what you want him to learn? The challenge is to be aware of the difficulty Mark faces. Be proactive in supporting him by making the environment right, drawing his attention to the focus at the start, enticing him to complete the task you want him to do before he draws yet another flag. Use techniques such as mind-maps to develop ways to help Mark get the main idea.

GETTING THE MAIN IDEA

It is not unusual for a pupil with autism to struggle with fine motor control and, consequently, to find written work a challenge. In addition to the slow, laborious style that means the pupil finds it difficult to complete tasks in a given time, the quality of the finished work often causes frustration. If you want your piece of work to look 'right' and it does not meet that standard, it is very easy to give up and just not want to bother.

Finding ways to enable the pupil to complete work when recording is a problem that requires flexibility and creativity on the part of the adults supporting the child. Rather than expecting the pupil to copy out whole sentences to fill in one or two missing words, photocopy the sentences and ask the pupil to write the missing words only. Consider the use of technology – a laptop or similar portable piece of equipment – to assist writing. If the task is to rearrange sentences into the right sequence, offer the option of cut and paste. Rather than providing a cluster of words to be matched and rewritten into pairs (opposites, for example), present the words in two lists to be joined by lines or arrows.

I can hear the protests! One reason for copying out is to stretch the task time in the lesson, keeping everyone under 'control'. This is not a reason to prevent a pupil from being successful in a task. Just keeping pupils busy for the sake of it impedes opportunities for further learning and does not stretch your pupils. If the pupil finishes before the end of the lesson, check out the next idea.

When lessons are not appropriately differentiated it is inevitable that pupils will finish their work at different times. What happens next? In some sessions, this is when chaos ensues because there isn't a contingency plan for what follows.

This is a difficult time for many pupils, but for an individual on the autistic spectrum two problems arise. First, if the pupil has not finished his work the distraction by others will make it impossible to carry on. Second, if the pupil does finish earlier than others he will struggle to know what to do unless this has been planned for and scheduled in. Without the structure, anxiety and insecurity will be raised and potential difficulties will arise.

To reduce these problems, ensure that the pupils know that if they finish the task before the end of the lesson there is something to move on to. This may include providing activities that link into the topic – word search or crosswords – or a selection of high interest/appropriate books available within the room. A file with personal material such as drawing paper, sticker collections and special interest information may be helpful, particularly if 'managed' by the pupil with an understanding that it can be used when work has been completed.

By building 'what's next' into the routine of the lesson we not only ensure better classroom management, we provide a subtle incentive to complete work in a timely manner.

I'VE FINISHED MY WORK, SIR

Praise and positive feedback usually motivate us to continue to apply ourselves well. Adults need praise and often crumble under criticism. We can't expect our pupils to react differently and, while we may go away and lick our wounds in private, an ASD pupil may react negatively on the spot.

On the other hand, some pupils on the spectrum do not want to become the centre of attention and would not thank you for praise or criticism. You may feel as if you can't win. The way to navigate this obstacle course is to get to know your pupils and find out what 'makes them tick'.

If through praise you see marked improvement, response, better application to the task and increased production, then praise some more. If you praise and see embarrassment, distraction from the task and inability to continue, then find another way to recognize the pupil's success. Do not just ignore the pupil.

There are many ways to offer praise, such as through writing a comment on the pupil's work or having a quiet word at the end of the lesson when he is leaving the room. Sometimes an indirect comment to the learning support assistant, if there is one, will take the attention away from the pupil and, of course, a simple 'thumbs-up' shared between you and the pupil can convey a very positive message.

Teachers are expected to set homework and most pupils accept it as an inevitable part of their education. As mentioned in Idea 49, it is often an area of conflict and confusion for pupils with ASD.

It is helpful in the first instance for the pupil to know what it is and why it is given. It is important for him to recognize the relationship between the homework and what happens in lessons. Taking the time to establish this can be helpful. A useful approach is to show the pupil how the two link by providing a visual schedule. For example, depicting the entire content of the week's work in mathematics:

Lesson 1	Lesson 2	Lesson 3	Homework
Monday	Wednesday	Friday	Friday

This not only demonstrates that the bulk of the work is done in school, but includes homework as part of the overall learning of mathematics.

Homework is usually given verbally at the end of the lesson when there are often distractions – packing up, checking timetables and general banter. If the pupil fails to hear the assignment he is unlikely to ask for it to be repeated and is then at a disadvantage. Try to alert the pupil by name to pay attention. Write the homework on the board or on a post-it note for the pupil to put in his diary. If the pupil is taking notes on the homework, allow adequate time for it to be written down and make yourself available to clarify the task if needed. It can be useful to use a peer to support the process.

MOTIVATION

We all find it difficult to be motivated at times and it is not unusual for any of us to lack motivation for things that seem to have no purpose. It is not uncommon for individuals with autism to lack motivation outside their area of special interest. When we recognize this difficulty as part of the pupil's ASD it becomes our responsibility to look at ways to develop interests and to become motivators.

Some principles to establish here interlink with previous ideas but need to be addressed in terms of the curriculum. It is important for you to be enthusiastic about the subject matter yourself by bringing it to life. Within the context of the topic, consider whether it is possible to link the work to the pupil's special interest. Be flexible in adapting the task to allow, for example, drawing rather than writing. Use the 'first . . . then . . .' approach as an incentive (see Idea 55) and help to clarify expectations by demonstrating a finished product, thus providing concrete, visual images to capture attention. Rather than expecting a sustained period of time on task, break the task down into small steps, with time to engage in the special interest between each step. Remember that no one is highly motivated by every activity every day and emphasize the priorities while being creative in the way the task is presented.

I have seen many models of individual education plans (IEPs) and it is probably fair to say that no two have been the same. This should be the case as the focus is meant to be on the individual. However, the similarity in many has been the targets that have been identified – targets related to the curriculum. If a pupil's identified special educational need is ASD, then the focus of the IEP should be on targets that address that need. Of course there is overlap with the curriculum and how to differentiate and deliver it, but if the triad of impairments – the social, communication and inflexibility issues – are not addressed, then the document does not reflect the pupil.

The IEP should be developed with parents, collaboratively writing targets that focus on the main areas for development. Some areas that may be addressed are participation in a small group, tolerance of a peer in a play situation or responding to a question when addressed by name. Other targets may concern the acceptance of new resources when introduced, remaining in the room for a set period of time, using a break card when anxious, or independently structuring the visual timetable at the start of the day.

If you can get these targets right, the pupil will be more able to access the curriculum and make academic progress.

IDEA

76

RECORD-KEEPING

Particularly in the early years, the majority of the work the child undertakes will be of a practical nature. It will not have the 'evidence' for success that is available when work is written and retained on paper and in exercise books. It is, nonetheless, important for there to be a record of what tasks the child is doing and what progress is being made.

○ Use a digital camera to record the child at work.
○ Build up a portfolio of work the child completes.
○ Use a recording sheet to indicate tasks and progress.

Date	Task	Comments	Staff initials
15.09.06	Sorting by colour	Success with two colours only	FB

Remember that progress is not just academic but should also include indicators such as time on task, generalization of a skill, social development, interaction, acceptance of change, awareness of others and so on. Celebrate all improvement and keep parents informed of the progress being made.

Tackling the curriculum

SPEAKING AND LISTENING

If communication is one of the areas of difficulty experienced by the pupil it is not surprising that aspects of English will create challenges. One of the anomalies that often confronts staff is the mismatch between expressive and receptive language. For example, a pupil with Asperger's syndrome may talk incessantly, particularly on a specialist topic, but may not be able to follow a conversation or participate in an exchange of dialogue. An assumption is then made that the pupil is not listening when in fact he does not understand the rules of social communication and is unable to get his head around the incoming message. This must be seen in light of processing time and literal understanding.

Another pupil with autism may have very little verbal communication and struggle to communicate at all. He may be able to pick up on context clues to follow instructions, and an assumption is made that the pupil has 'understood' what was said.

Here are some ways to help this situation.

○ Help the pupil to remain on a given topic and draw him back to this topic if moving onto special interests.
○ Recognize the difference between expressive and receptive language and ensure that you are making yourself clearly understood.
○ Reduce your language to key words to emphasize the main message you are attempting to convey.

It is not uncommon for the pupil to have a mismatch between reading and comprehending. Frequently a pupil on the autistic spectrum will be an excellent decoder of language, reading fluently and with ease, and yet not have comprehended what has been read. The two skills are not equal. Again, an assumption is made that the pupil is deliberately being difficult when the problem is genuine and must be addressed.

It is important to assess the pupil's reading and comprehension and provide appropriately differentiated work to meet the individual needs. Patiently help the pupil to make the links between reading and understanding what has been read by drawing him back to the text to look for the answers. It's a good idea to pair the pupil with a peer who has difficulty with decoding but who has strong comprehension skills.

When you are checking for comprehension, rather than ask, for example, 'What did Mr Thomas eat for breakfast?', rephrase the question to say, 'Look for the sentence about Mr Thomas eating breakfast' and then pose the question itself. Avoid embarrassing the pupil by asking him to answer a comprehension question in front of the group unless this has been written down first.

It is also worth noting that some pupils with autism prefer factual reading material to fiction and may find it easier to understand. Offering options where possible may enhance performance.

BUT I DON'T UNDERSTAND

CREATIVE WRITING

Difficulties with imagination and flexibility will have an inevitable impact on the pupil's ability to respond to imaginative and creative writing. This will also create some tension in response to questions such as, 'What do you think will happen next?'

To support the pupil with this challenge:

o provide visual supports – photographs, drawings, picture books, video clips – to create the ideas

o provide a range of options in response to, 'What do you think . . .' in order to demonstrate to the pupil that there is no one right answer

o offer the opportunity for the pupil to draw diagrams or pictures prior to written work or in place of written work

o praise positive attempts in order to raise confidence.

Although not always the case, mathematics can be an area of strength for some pupils on the autistic spectrum because it is built on logic. Rote learning is easier to master than concepts, and the 'problem solving' and verbal reasoning demands that are presented often impede success. If the pupil struggles with sequencing, working with number can also be a challenge.

To help the pupil:

○ support learning with concrete materials
○ link work to the pupil's special interest where possible, for example, if the special interest is cars, use cars for counting, sorting, matching, comparing
○ develop life skills by using money (real, not plastic), weights and measures generalized to/from food technology
○ practise mathematical skills across different areas – buying snacks and lunch, organizing the bus fare
○ teach mathematics skills through games and activities to develop concepts without relying on worksheets and exercise books
○ consider the layout of work on a page, ensuring clarity of presentation
○ regularly revisit concepts to ensure learning is retained.

MATHEMATICS

The difficulties the pupil experiences with imagination may create frustration when he is asked to predict and hypothesize in science lessons. To help the pupil in science consider:

o carefully choosing a peer for paired work
o repeating the same experiment to enable success in predicting the *second* time
o using a video or digital photographs as a slide show to analyse what took place
o designing a clearly structured form for writing up experiments
o providing visual support through diagrams
o linking into the environment and life experiences, where possible.

Be alert to sensory issues such as odour, temptation to taste and tactile defensiveness with materials. You also need to be aware of risks related to heath and safety through inexperience with substances and a lack of awareness of danger.

PHYSICAL EDUCATION

While you will find some of your pupils on the autistic spectrum agile and active, others will have difficulty with gross motor skills, may be awkward in movement and poorly coordinated. In addition to these challenges, the socialization issues and lack of interaction with peers make involvement in team sports very difficult. It is no wonder that some of these pupils become anxious in PE and often opt out.

To encourage participation, select a small group of peers who will engage with the pupil patiently and model the skills being introduced. Relying on verbal instructions for an activity will often lead to failure.

If the pupil lacks confidence and is self-conscious in the lesson, do not put him on the spot to demonstrate an action.

Choose a role that the pupil can do well. It may be that while the peer group plays football, the pupil with autism can record data such as shots on goal and substitutions. Providing a useful role helps him to feel included while eliminating the anxiety of full participation.

Given the problems with being an active part of the group, try putting a positive focus on personal fitness, challenging the pupil to set targets and break his own records. Such activities can lead to interests being carried on outside school and into adult life.

Remember that fitness can be achieved without expecting the pupil to join in with activities that may never bring a sense of accomplishment and that heighten anxiety.

THE ARTS

It is not uncommon for the general public to expect individuals with autism to show exceptional talent, often in the areas of the arts and music. In reality these special gifts are present in only a small percentage of people on the spectrum. When such ability does exist it is innate and enables the person to achieve highly in a very specialist area that is usually not generalized to other aspects of daily life.

For the majority of your pupils, however, the arts may pose their own difficulties related to the limits of imagination and difficulties with motor control. If one cannot visualize, it follows that skills requiring creativity will be a struggle. There may also be difficulties related to sensory issues of texture and odour when the pupil comes into contact with art and design materials. He may also be sensitive to sounds in music.

To support the pupil:

○ encourage use of skills in a safe environment
○ offer a range of opportunities to explore materials
○ remember that the pupil may find it difficult to express opinions about art and artists
○ use visual stimuli to heighten interest and support work
○ be aware of sensory reaction to resources and materials, for example, in music, consider volume and use of headphones
○ use the lessons to support skills such as turn-taking and peer interaction.

In its own right, music can be a valuable tool for developing communication and gaining the pupil's attention. It can bring pleasure and relaxation as well as enhancing interaction. Be alert to the response of the pupil and tap into the wider opportunities that the arts can provide.

For many pupils with autism ICT is not only an area where success is achieved but is also a motivator and can be a useful tool in developing other areas of the curriculum through computer-assisted learning. It is often easier to follow instructions delivered visually on the monitor than to understand human instruction. However, it can also become an all-consuming interest where the pupil will want to do his own thing rather than focus on the lesson content delivered by the teacher.

Using technology can also assist communication, as some pupils will interact with others by email and through chat rooms more confidently than face to face.

To support ICT:

- ○ consider using 'first . . . (the work required), then . . . (the pupil's choice)' to develop time on task
- ○ encourage work with a peer (taking turns, developing a task together) to develop interaction
- ○ praise skills
- ○ provide opportunities for the pupil to demonstrate strengths to others
- ○ select programs that will support the development of the curriculum in a user-friendly manner.

IDEA

85

It is not unusual for pupils on the autistic spectrum to have strong memories relating to their own experiences, remembering dates and places accurately. At the same time there may be little or no understanding of 'history' as in past times and past cultures. Rote learning of the facts may be strong, but if asked to write about the life of a child in another era the task would be virtually impossible. In order to foster understanding:

○ use mind-maps to make links (see Idea 64)
○ develop a timeline to represent visually the passage of time (for a young child the timeline can be represented by photographs from infancy to the present)
○ use photographs and paintings to spark interest in writing
○ bring the period to life with clips from videos and DVDs
○ use photographs of now and then to spot the differences, prompting as necessary
○ use artefacts and visits to places of interest to build concrete understanding.

Like any area of the curriculum, learning in geography is built up from early foundation skills. From a young age pupils are engaged in 'mapping' skills through learning routes around their school and community. They learn about weather through the daily symbols and songs as part of classroom routine. These early skills are then broadened over the years to cover the curriculum at the different Key Stages.

Some pupils on the autistic spectrum may show disinterest in this area of the curriculum and see it as irrelevant. On the other hand, some may take on a special interest, such as earthquakes or an individual nation, and become the 'expert' on the topic. It is important that information is built on what the pupil already knows – from the foundation of the local community and routes around school to national and global awareness. Try to move them from rain, sun and wind symbols to weather patterns and climates. As with other areas of learning:

o base presentations on visual prompts
o draw on the experiences of the pupil
o make links to the cultural diversity represented within the group
o demonstrate using the senses, for example, tasting foods from different world areas and learning why they grow there
o tap into the special interest of the pupil and use this to link to other topics. For example, if the pupil is passionate about local trains, investigate the development of train travel in the area of the world being studied.

Be creative about your subject, inject enthusiasm and support the pupil step by step.

Personal, social and health education (PSHE) is relevant across the school day and weaves in and out of other areas of the curriculum. It supports the development of essential life skills, such as respect for others, socialization, coping with disappointment and developing flexibility. In this respect, PSHE can and should be a tool to support the pupil with ASD across the day.

Within the context of all lessons PSHE is being addressed through encouraging independence and instilling confidence in the pupil. Activities that underpin this focus should include opportunities to compare similarities and differences in pupils' appearance, interests and skills, along with helping the pupil to recognize his own strengths and weaknesses as well as those of others. These activities can be organized with the use of peer observation sheets and peer interviews in an interactive session facilitated by a teacher or learning support assistant.

Providing opportunities for conflict resolution in a safe environment is also an important aspect of PSHE. By introducing a controversial topic – for example, the pros and cons of school uniforms – and enabling pupils to present differing sides of the argument, you are able to introduce the democratic process and present the idea of 'agreeing to disagree'. This provides a model of what regularly occurs in day-to-day life and can promote the skills of mediation when misunderstanding occurs, mutual respect and relationship-building.

Given the difficulties pupils on the autistic spectrum often have with understanding facial expression, gesture and body language, PSHE sessions can provide opportunities to role-play scenarios where peers act out emotions while others interpret the emotion itself along with the possible reason for the behaviours being demonstrated. Opportunities to reflect on images of, say, anger, frustration or annoyance in a safe environment can be beneficial to heightening awareness. This can also be used to address issues of vulnerability and bullying, seeking to identify what bullying is and why it occurs.

PSHE can also provide opportunities to learn about healthy choices in diet and exercise, linking in to PE and food technology as well as daily life. Exploring the range of options in these two areas of development can introduce new choices and help the pupil to recognize the need for broadening his horizon.

Each of these skills is an essential part of everyday life and any opportunities that can develop understanding and tolerance are worth capitalizing on.

MODERN FOREIGN LANGUAGES

It is not uncommon for pupils with special educational needs to be exempted from learning a modern foreign language to receive additional support in core subjects. While this may be an option with some pupils on the autistic spectrum, it should not be assumed that languages are inaccessible to these pupils without proper assessment. As many pupils with autism are good mimics they are sometimes fascinated by a different accent and the new vocabulary presented. If this is the case, the subject could be seen as a strength and could offer future opportunities for development. To maximize success:

○ use a picture dictionary approach to illustrate vocabulary

○ provide videos or DVDs to emphasize dialogue and accent

○ when emphasizing speech with gesture and body language be aware that the pupil may find this difficult to understand.

If, on the other hand, the pupil's communication needs are such that spoken language is difficult at all times, vocabulary is weak and word-finding skills are a challenge, it may be worth excusing him from learning a modern foreign language and using this time to provide discrete sessions for one of the areas of weakness he experiences.

Working with others can be a real challenge for pupils with autism. The difficulties of accepting the perspective of another and the tendency to see only one way of doing something cause the pupil to struggle in this setting. The pace of the discussion can also be difficult for the pupil to follow and, as peers often speak without the clarity of an adult, some of their contributions are missed completely. In the end, the pupil may be totally disengaged. He may find it difficult to ask questions and to follow the flow of conversation.

These barriers, however, should not mean that we give up on including him in group work. It is important to consider the size of the group and reduce the number appropriate to the pupil's needs. If discrete skills are being taught, some of these should include how a group functions and give the pupil some keys to success. A visual reminder may also be of benefit to others in the group and by using it generally the pupil with autism will not be singled out.

When I am in a group I will try to:

- Listen to others when they speak.
- Wait my turn to speak.
- Speak loudly enough for others to hear me.
- Ask for help if I do not understand.

A pupil on the autistic spectrum will often be allocated a number of hours of support throughout the week. This ranges from limited time for specific sessions to full time if required. High levels of support can be beneficial for the pupil but can also, over time, impede his development of independence. Unfortunately, some learning support assistants become 'joined at the hip' with the pupil. They see the need before it arises and wait on the pupil hand and foot. Their presence reduces the child's need to ask for help, to problem solve and to engage with peers. In part, the difficulty is that an assistant feels lax in his/her duties if not attached to the child, and the role becomes one of preventing the ASD pupil from disrupting the class group and teacher.

The role must be one of balance and there are some key issues for the support assistant to focus on.

o Liaise with teachers to prepare the pupil for change and new topics.
o Get to know the pupil's strengths and weaknesses.
o Set small tasks and withdraw, allowing the pupil to work independently for increasing lengths of time.
o Work across the group, returning to the assigned pupil as necessary.
o Work within a small group, prompting the pupil to wait for his turn.
o Draw the pupil's attention to what is happening away from his immediate space.
o Generalize the pupil's learning into new situations within and outside the classroom.
o Encourage peers to point out information and engage with the pupil.

Developing the appropriate way to support the pupil will be based on an understanding of his needs. The training of staff is vital, through ASD-specific courses, reading appropriate books to develop understanding and sharing good practice with others who have experience of working with pupils on the autistic spectrum.

There may come a time when the ASD pupil will be faced with examinations. If the pupil is able and has achieved well academically, the content will not be the main difficulty here. It is more likely that anxiety will build as a result of the changes in routine.

To support the pupil and help him to succeed:

o identify the best time for study and preparation
o identify who is best able to help the pupil prepare
o be realistic about expectations and the level of work to be examined
o help the pupil develop a clear timetable for the examination period and ensure that he has one at home as well as at school
o help the pupil to develop relaxation techniques
o prepare the pupil in advance. For example, if the hall is to become the examination room, explain this and show him the arrangement of the room before the examinations begin
o carefully manage where the pupil should sit – near an exit? At the front without the distraction of others ahead? At the back to observe the posture and silence of others?
o consider an alternative environment
o decide if extra time is required
o praise the pupil's ability prior to the start of the examination
o be available at the end to support as necessary.

Change is a major cause of anxiety, so it is vital that the pupil is well prepared for the examination routines. Your sensitive management and support can make a real difference.

EXAMINATIONS

Facing the challenge of change

IDEA

92

ENCOURAGE FLEXIBILITY

While most of us take change in our stride, a major feature in the lives of pupils with autism is the difficulty of accepting change and being flexible. This can have an impact on all areas of daily life, including what is worn or eaten, the route to a destination, the change of a schedule and the people along the way. There is security in sameness that is undermined by change.

Because of our own flexibility we struggle to understand this need for consistency, the need to be warned of impending change and the anxiety that results when preparation is not made for this. We want to respond with 'Lighten up' or 'It's no big deal'. But, you see, it is a big deal when uncertainty and change create anxiety and fear.

So, what do we do to encourage flexibility? First we need to identify the most difficult situations faced by the pupil. Once identified, we need to find small ways to help him manage unexpected change.

Consider this example. James goes swimming with his class every week. He is relaxed and looks forward to getting to the local baths. Every week the coach takes the same route to the baths, a route James has come to know well. But, alas, one week there is a diversion as the result of road works. The coach has to turn right earlier than usual. James becomes anxious and begins to scream, getting out of his seat and endangering himself and others. Why? James no longer knows that he is going to the baths. He knows one route. He does not have the confidence to know that the driver is able to find another way there. He assumes they are not going swimming after all and that he will miss the activity he enjoys.

How can James be supported to react differently next time? One thing that can be used is a Social Story™ (see Idea 51) to show that there are many ways to get to one place. Looking at a map of the local area and identifying the different ways to get to the baths may also be helpful. If the change is known in advance it should be explained to James, and reassurance offered. If it is not known ahead of time the reassurance needs to be offered within the situation. Never belittle the pupil's fear when an unexpected change occurs, but do try to help him to resolve the issue.

Resistance to change can make daily tasks much more challenging for the pupil. It raises barriers to learning and living. Sometimes it is necessary to help the pupil accept options and to develop a degree of flexibility by carefully sabotaging a situation.

Anne loved food technology, primarily because she loved to eat the finished product. This was a true motivator and participation was very good in lessons. Until . . . the day we were making a cake with butter as one of the ingredients and we only had margarine. This was *not* acceptable – the recipe said butter – and as a result Anne refused to participate, was angry that the lesson did not stop for a trip to the shops to get the butter, and made her anger felt.

What did we do? Others in the group made the cake and Anne was offered a piece to eat. As it looked edible Anne agreed to taste it and she liked it. A discussion then took place about why we could substitute one thing for another, in this case margarine for butter.

In future lessons, sabotage was deliberately planned by explaining to Anne, for example, that we did not have soft brown sugar but we had demerara sugar and we would try that. As time went on Anne was encouraged to suggest different things that could be substituted, and huge strides in acceptance were made.

Rather than accept the inflexibility it is important that the pupil has the opportunity to develop new ways of looking at options.

SABOTAGE

A RANGE OF RESOURCES

When the difficulties of generalization and inflexibility are combined, the pupil with autism faces an amazing challenge. If you only see an object as the one you were first introduced to – the thick blue pencil, for example – and the object is lost, you are faced with a dilemma. If you have learned to weigh on a kitchen scale in food technology and are presented with a different model in science, what do you do? If you know what it means to 'join the back of the queue' but the teacher tells you to stand at the back of the line, where do you go?

Recognizing the difficulties faced by the pupil should challenge us to use resources, human and inanimate, to broaden understanding and reduce resistance to change.

o Take time to explain when confusion occurs.
o Be alert to difficulty and confusion when it arises.
o Help the pupil to recognize a range of equipment identified by function – scales, rulers, scissors, cutlery, pens.
o Explain phrases that have generally the same meaning, such as sit down and sit up straight.
o Use different staff to support the pupil, reducing reliance on one and rejection of others.

There will always be changes that arise where we are unable to warn the pupil in advance. However, there are many situations within the day when we have the monopoly of information and we need to be sensitive to the need for the young person to be informed. Actually, we don't always react positively to the unpredictable ourselves. If we find out at midday that the head has called a staff meeting after school, we may react negatively. We may also worry that the unplanned-for meeting is going to deliver bad news and the rest of the day is spent with raised anxiety. If we had known about the meeting, if it had been on the schedule, we would be fine.

What kind of things do we often know in advance and for which we are able to prepare the pupil? Change of rooms, supply staff, a future INSET day, the cancellation of a lesson and a new topic to be introduced are examples of change to which we should be able to alert the pupil. When we fail to do this, we are contributing to the anxiety that the pupil will experience.

The responsibility to warn of change will vary across situations. There may be a support assistant who works closely with the pupil who helps to manage his timetable. If so, close liaison with other staff will be essential, enabling the assistant to be aware of the change. The assistant should have a system to communicate the changes to the pupil, for example, a set time to brief at the start of the day, a central communication noticeboard, a telephone call to home the previous evening. It may be the form tutor who takes the responsibility at the start of the day by having a designated space on the whiteboard or classroom door to 'announce' changes for the day. In some situations it will be the subject teacher who will need to give warning of change. Once again it must be emphasized that whole-school understanding and responsibility are essential to foster success.

BENDING THE RULES

Inflexibility and resistance to change have an impact on the ability of the pupil with autism to respond to the school rules and to the 'rules of the game'. As has been established in previous ideas, rules that emphasize what to do rather than what not to do often have a stronger influence. But it is not just the understanding of the rules that can be difficult. The fact is, we often change or relax the rules if everyone agrees.

Some examples may help to clarify this. Many schools have strict uniform rules that must be followed by all pupils. Then, almost without warning, a non-uniform day is held. Other pupils in the school celebrate the freedom and diversity that this brings, but not the ASD pupil. He is left bewildered and may very well arrive at school in uniform. If not in uniform the pupil may be out of sorts, feeling that this should not be happening and the confusion of the change of rules can lead to anxiety. Similarly, when a teacher has a strict seating arrangement in a class and the pupils take advantage of a supply teacher by moving to different positions, for most this is a good joke, but for the pupil on the spectrum it is confusing and distressing. It is especially difficult for peers to understand a pupil who reacts negatively to such changes.

This is a very difficult problem to solve and can only be addressed through patient explanation and discrete teaching to help the pupil recognize that rules are *usually* to be kept but that *sometimes* they can be broken. When situations of this nature arise it is essential to warn in advance and explain the need to accept the change. The responsible adult in the situation must be proactive in recognizing when explanations are required and when intervention is necessary.

It might be helpful to identify some scenarios for discussion with the pupil:

The rule	Can it be broken?	When?	Why?
30 mph	yes	In emergency	Police, fire, ambulance access
Swearing at a teacher	no	never	There are other ways to cope with anger and frustration
School uniform	yes	On non-uniform days	Raising money for charity, everyone agreed

NEGOTIATION

Too often we fall into the trap of thinking that a quick 'Don't worry about it' will relax the pupil and help him to carry on as normal. This is unlikely to happen and we must be prepared to spend the time negotiating change. This skill does not come naturally to everyone and in the case of supporting a child on the autistic spectrum success is more likely when the adult concerned has a positive relationship with the pupil.

Change is an inevitable part of life and if we fail to give the pupil the tools to cope with some of the changes he will face we reduce the possibility of future independence.

Let's take the example of a pupil who cannot face attending a lesson if a supply teacher is covering for an absent member of staff. The pupil may have opted out of the situation in the past by going to the library or SEN department rather than the lesson and wants to be able to continue this. This can lead to lost learning time and further difficulty catching up with what was taught during this time. The member of staff may be off for a period of time, increasing the problem.

How do we negotiate with the pupil to attend the lesson? If possible, forewarn the pupil of the change as well as putting supply staff in perspective by explaining that they are part of the staff team. Assure the pupil that the supply teacher knows the subject and reassure the pupil in terms of those aspects of the lesson that will be the same. His concerns must be explained to the supply teacher.

Unfortunately, there are times when the atmosphere of the class changes dramatically when the regular teacher is not present. This is a school issue that needs to be addressed for the sake of all pupils, not just those on the autistic spectrum. If there were questions about safety and vulnerability, decisions would need to be made in light of this.

We have all learned so much by watching others respond to situations. Many of us can probably name our role models, the people who have influenced the way we have developed. This, in itself, is not an easy thing for people on the autistic spectrum to do. The incidental learning is often missing.

This does not, however, preclude us from demonstrating the right way to respond to change. Sometimes we are more inflexible than we care to admit and can be reinforcing the behaviour of our pupils. To show a pupil how to cope with change it is important to analyse what has gone wrong and how the situation could have been managed more positively. Using this information you can then replay the event and offer the pupil a menu of responses. He may not choose the most ideal, but this gives an opportunity to analyse the new choice and move on to another. Along with this, there will be times when the change is related to you and this is an opportunity to point this out to the pupil as in, 'I was supposed to be on a break but Mrs Smith had to leave so I'll have to stay here. I don't like change but it can't be helped. I'll take my break later.' Too frequently we react negatively to change and seldom give the pupil examples of how we cope with it.

IDEA

98

SHOW ME HOW

FRUSTRATIONS

We often fall into the trap of thinking that the frustration is ours because we do not easily solve the problems of the pupil with autism. To a degree this is true but if we turn this around and recognize that the real frustration is for the pupil because of our lack of understanding it creates a new perspective.

If you must be frustrated, let this result in positive energy to recognize the confusion of the pupil and your general lack of understanding about the complexity of ASD. Turn your focus to problem solving to get to the bottom of the pupil's dilemma and find creative ways to support development. Analyse the situation in the following terms, first acknowledging your frustration and then turning it to look at the situation through the eyes of the pupil.

You see the frustration as:	The pupil has the frustration of:
Challenging behaviour	Not knowing what the expectations are
Not getting through	Being overwhelmed with mixed messages and sensory overload
Lack of will to learn	Not understanding the instructions

When you begin to gain the perspective of the pupil your frustration will be converted into a longing to support.

At each stage of transition within the ongoing development of a pupil on the autistic spectrum additional planning and organization will need to be considered. The huge upheaval of leaving a known environment where routines have been established and relationships built and starting afresh can be fraught with anxiety and tension.

Discussion on transition to follow secondary school must begin in Year 9 when the pupil is 14 years old. The Connexions service is responsible for overseeing the delivery of the transition plan once it has been drawn up at the Year 9 review. As with any other pupils, a range of options must be considered, including sixth form in the secondary school, sixth-form college, college of further education, other vocational or occupational training. A further option may be a specialist residential college if the pupil's needs are best met in this context.

The transition review draws together information from a range of individuals who know the pupil best and focuses on beyond school and into adult life. The views of the pupil must be sought and if the pupil finds it difficult to communicate his views they must be represented.

It is essential that:

o planning is done well in advance
o visits are made at various times of the day in the new environment
o staff in the new situation are fully briefed on the needs of the pupil
o transition is supported by those who know the pupil best.

Without thoughtful planning and the investment of time a new placement can too easily break down and result in anguish for the pupil and his family.

TRANSITION AND BEYOND

APPENDIX

You will find a wealth of information available to
further your understanding of pupils on the
autistic spectrum. The following is a partial list of
recommended reading and websites and each, in turn,
will lead you to further links. Enjoy your journey of
investigation and learning.

READING

○ *Asperger's Syndrome: A Guide for Parents and
Professionals* by Tony Atwood, (Jessica Kingsley
Publishers, 1997)

○ *Inclusion in the primary classroom: support materials for
children with autistic spectrum disorders* by Joy Beaney
and Penny Kershaw (The National Autistic Society,
2003)

○ *Developing Inclusive School Practice: A Practical Guide*
by Rita Cheminais (David Fulton Publishers, 2001)

○ *Asperger Syndrome: A Practical Guide for Teachers* by
Val Cumine, Julia Leach and Gill Stevenson (David
Fulton Publishers, 1998)

○ *My Social Stories Book* by Carol Gray (Jessica
Kingsley Publishers, 2002)

○ *Thinking in Pictures* by Temple Grandin (Vintage
Books, 1996, updated 2006)

○ *Freaks, Geeks & Asperger Syndrome* by Luke Jackson
(Jessica Kingsley Publishers, 2002)

○ *Accessing the Curriculum for Pupils with Autistic
Spectrum Disorders* by Gary Mesibov and Marie
Howley (David Fulton Publishers, 2003)

○ *Autistic Spectrum Disorders in the Early Years: A Guide
for Practitioners* by Rita Jordan (QEd, 2002)

○ *Understanding and Teaching Children with Autism* by
Rita Jordan and Stuart Powell (Wiley, 1995)

○ *Making it a Success: Practical Strategies and Worksheets
for Teaching Students with Autism Spectrum Disorder* by
Sue Larkey (Jessica Kingsley Publishers, 2005)

○ *Understanding and Working with the Spectrum of
Autism* by Wendy Lawson (Jessica Kingsley
Publishers, 2001)

- *Guidelines for working with pupils with an ASD in Key Stages 3 and 4* by South Gloucestershire Council (National Autistic Society, 2005)
- *The sensory world of the autistic spectrum: a greater understanding* (National Autistic Society, 2005)
- *Martian in the playground* by Clare Sainsbury (Lucky Duck Publishing Ltd, 2000)
- *Autistic Spectrum Disorder, Positive Approaches for Teaching Children with ASD* by Diana Seach (NASEN, Tamworth, 1998)
- *The Autistic Spectrum: A Guide for Parents and Professionals* by Lorna Wing (Constable and Robinson, 2003, 2nd edition)
- *Autistic Spectrum Disorders: Good Practice Guidance* (Department for Education and Skills, Department of Health DfES/597/2002/REV)
- *The Curious Incident of the Dog in the Night-time* by Mark Haddon (Random House, 2003)

USEFUL INFORMATION

- National Autistic Society – www.nas.org.uk
- Autism Awareness – www.autism-awareness.org.uk
- PECS – the Picture Exchange Communication System – www.pecs.org.uk
- Social Stories™ – www.thegraycenter.org
- TEACCH – Treatment and Education of Autistic and Related Communication Handicapped Children – www.teacch.com